The Reader Revealed

The Reader Revealed

Compiled and edited by Sabrina Alcorn Baron

with Elizabeth Walsh and Susan Scola

The Folger
Shakespeare Library
Washington, DC
2001

Distributed by University
of Washington Press
Seattle and London

This volume has been published in conjunction with
the exhibition *The Reader Revealed*, presented at
The Folger Shakespeare Library,® Washington, DC,
from September 4, 2001, through January 19, 2002.

Werner Gundersheimer
Director

Richard Kuhta
Librarian

Rachel Doggett
Andrew W. Mellon Curator of Books and Exhibitions

The exhibition and the catalogue have been funded
by The Winton and Carolyn Blount Exhibition Fund
of The Folger Shakespeare Library.

Distributed by University of Washington Press,
Seattle and London.
ISBN 0-295-98183-0

Photographs by Julie Ainsworth.

Inside cover:
Jan van der Straet (1523–1605).
Spectacle maker (detail).
Engraving by Jan Collaert, from *Noua Reperta*.
Antwerp, ca. 1600.

Design by Studio A, Alexandria, VA.

Printing by Hagerstown Bookbinding and Printing,
Hagerstown, MD.

Contents

Foreword

Books are such an integral part of every facet of our lives that, even as we wonder about their future, we easily forget how precious they were to early modern readers. The close relationship between reader and book, between reading and writing, during the fifteenth, sixteenth, and seventeenth centuries has left us with a large body of evidence not only of the habits of individual readers but of the social and intellectual worlds they inhabited. Thanks in no small part to Henry Clay Folger and his penchant for books that were "rather soiled by use," the Folger Shakespeare Library is uniquely situated to introduce today's readers to those of the past.

We are grateful to Sabrina Alcorn Baron who, assisted by Elizabeth Walsh and Susan Scola, assembled a rich and varied group of books, manuscripts, and works of art for *The Reader Revealed*. She and her associates have brought to life the early owners and readers of many Folger books, from the humble and pious to the most assiduous collectors. Steven N. Zwicker, whose groundbreaking research has directed our attention to the recoverable evidence of early modern reading, was the first to suggest such an exhibition. He has generously provided ideas and guidance throughout the project. Thanks also go to Anthony Grafton, Evelyn B. Tribble, Arthur F. Marotti, Kevin Sharpe, Jennifer Andersen, Anna Battigelli, and William H. Sherman, whose essays in this catalogue contribute greatly to our portrait of the early modern reader.

Every book in the Folger collection is unique. Every one has passed through different hands and has accumulated its own particular history. We can study that history in part because early modern readers did what readers in the Folger Library may not do: they read with pen in hand. It is in their underlinings, emendations, and other marginalia that these readers are most vividly revealed to us. As we look to the future and ponder the question, "Whither the book?," we must also ask "Whither readers and writers?" These questions have a particular resonance for me as I hold a pen for the first time in six weeks after recovering from a broken arm. The shelves of the Folger Library have yielded far more glimpses into the lives and thoughts of early modern readers than we could manage to display. As we prepared the exhibition, our hands touched the pages that others touched and annotated centuries ago. Dependent on keyboard, mechanical printer, and electronic texts, I cannot help wondering whether tomorrow's historians will have as rich an archive to mine, whether our thoughts and questions, our despair and delight with what we read, will come to life as vibrantly as those of the readers revealed here.

Rachel Doggett
Andrew W. Mellon Curator of Books and Exhibitions

Acknowledgments

The definition of "collaboration" should read "mounting an exhibition accompanied by a catalogue." Over the course of four years, *The Reader Revealed* received assistance and cooperation from scholars on three continents. The original concept for an exhibition addressing readers and their books grew out of a 1997 NEH Summer Institute at the Folger on "Habits of Reading in Early Modern England" conducted by Steven N. Zwicker. Steve embraces scholars and scholarship from all fields in an effort to construct an accurate and vital picture of the past. His work and his welcome are inspiration for numerous scholars around the globe. Rachel Doggett, Curator of Books and Exhibitions at the Folger, was enthusiastic from the start. Her intimate knowledge of the Folger collections, coupled with that of Elizabeth Walsh, Head of Reader Services, are unsurpassed as resources. They contributed immeasurably to the range and quality of materials on display, and to all other aspects of this project. The enthusiasm and organizational skills of Susan Scola, assistant to the Curator of Books, were central in getting this exhibition off the ground. In addition, the cheerful and efficient assistance and flexibility of Rosalind Larry, LuEllen DeHaven, and the entire Reading Room staff were vital to all aspects of the project. Kathleen Lynch, Executive Director of the Folger Institute, and Anthony Grafton, of Princeton University, generously consulted and shared ideas linking the exhibition, catalogue, and conference on "Transactions of the Book" (1–3 November 2001).

Frank Mowery, Head of Conservation, and his colleagues Linda Blaser and Linda Hohneke provided ideas and designs for the exhibition. Julie Ainsworth, Head of Photography, produced the beautiful photographs for the catalogue. The Library of Catholic University of America, Washington, DC; Peter W. M. Blayney, of Toronto, Canada; Saint John's University, Collegeville, MN; and Pilgrim Hall Museum, Plymouth, MA, graciously lent items to the exhibition, and Heritage Bookshop generously donated leaves of the Pennyroyal-Caxton Bible. Thanks are due also to the contributors of the essays in this catalogue, who were a great group to work with, prompt and responsive to the last. Suellen Towers and Josh McKeon, rare book catalogers at the Folger, pointed out many items of interest, and Georgianna Zielger, Head of Reference Services, kindly shared her work on Esther Inglis. In addition, thanks to Erin Blake, Heather Wolfe, Laetitia Yeandle, Marilyn Barth, Barbara Henry, Karin Goldstein, Elizabeth L. Eisenstein, Lyn Tribble, Lori Ann Ferrell, Stuart Sherman, Peter Stallybrass, Linda Levy Peck, Carol Brobeck, Frederic Baron, Eleanor Shevlin, Janis Hill, Julie Biggs, and Mary Tonkinson for their contributions. The ultimate thanks should go to Henry Clay Folger whose legacy has made the knowledge of generations of readers, past, present, and future, possible and tangible.

Sabrina Alcorn Baron
Takoma Park, MD

Detail from Agostino Ramelli, *Le diverse et artificiose machine*, Paris, 1588.
Folger call no. TJ 144 R2 1588 Cage.

The Reader Revealed

Steven N. Zwicker

If you stand at the corner of East Capitol and Second Street in Washington, DC—the Folger Library to one side, the Library of Congress to the other—you might think that you were at the center of the world of books. Here it would be possible to write a history of the book, and that is exactly what a number of scholars—of literature; of social, political, and intellectual history; of editing, publishing, and collecting; of bookbinding, typography, and paper conservation—have been doing for the past decade and more. They have joined with scholars around the world in a superb feat of intellectual archaeology, a reconstruction of the history, or rather of the many histories, of the book as the central instrument of intellectual life for the past five hundred years. Nor has it escaped their notice that writing the history of the book at a time when electronic technologies are at once transforming and threatening the life of the book has given that history a sense of urgency, and perhaps a touch of melancholy. It might even seem as if scholars had gotten around to the history of the book only when the book was threatened with extinction, and though that sense of timing is not quite accurate, the near simultaneity has sharpened our attentiveness to the life of the book in all of its material and institutional complexity. At the same time, technologies of the internet have made us newly aware of the ways in which information is stored, retrieved, displayed, and consumed. The history of the book has come to a full flowering at a point where, computer in hand, we have all become connoisseurs of consumption, and writing that history in the age of the internet has evoked, perhaps demanded, yet another story, not of production, but of consumption, a history, that is, of readers and reading.

The books of the Folger Library, of the Library of Congress, and of similar collections around the world give us a vivid sense of the richness of the archive for the historian of the book. Even though only a small percentage of the books produced in the past has survived, the problem for the historian of the book might seem rather a surfeit than a lack of evidence. Readers and reading are quite another matter. Reading, like other acts of consumption—like eating, looking, or listening—seems to deny its material premise. Once we have finished holding the book in our hands, we remove our body from the act and the event vanishes without a trace. To construct a history of reading might seem then a nearly impossible task: we read by ourselves; we read lying in bed or in the bath; we read in studies, offices, or libraries; we read passively, privately, and silently. But the early modern reader was likely none of these things, and we can begin to gather a sense of that reader equipped for reading, 'studied for action,' surrounded by books, contemplating and marking texts—from the superb portraits that Holbein made of Erasmus and Thomas More, or that Quentin Metsys made of Peter Gilles, or that Lady Anne Clifford commissioned of herself amidst her books. The early modern theater is also a revealing and emblematic site for readers and reading—"*Enter Hamlet reading on a Booke*"; "Read on this book, / That show of such an exercise may colour / Your loneliness." Perhaps most revealing of all is the material evidence left by readers themselves, for the early modern reader was an epitome of material action—studious, attentive, and composed. Armed with pen and penknife; with ink and inkhorn; with sand and sandbox; with letter cases and paper; with table books, journals, and commonplace books, early modern readers left their traces everywhere: on the covers of books, on title pages, on flyleaves and pastedowns, all over the margins of books, even between lines of print.

Indeed, the intimacy of reading and writing throughout the early modern period has left us with a crucial archive for constructing a history of reading in that world. While it is true that reading and writing were taught separately in the early modern period, and it is certainly the case that some early modern readers were not writers, it is equally true that writing was among the most visible and widespread habits of early modern reading. To read with pen in hand underscoring or otherwise marking memorable passages; to correct errors or emend the text and cite variant readings; to gloss or interline with technical or rhetorical terms or with translations and citations; to summarize and cross-refer; to outline and paraphrase; to make synopses and provide interpretations; to extract maxims from Scripture and sermons, from plays and poems, from prayers and devotions; to move themes, arguments, and topics, indeed whole poems, elegies, and epitaphs, recipes and remedies, speeches and letters from one transcript to another, from printed book or manuscript text to commonplace compilation, notebook, or miscellany—these were indeed among the most commonplace acts of the early modern reader.

Such signs of reading are to be found repeatedly in early modern printed books and manuscripts. At times they are made by owners dating and otherwise marking their books; sometimes by multiple owners who occasionally respond to earlier marking. Books have come down to us that were shared within families, passed from husband to wife, and from one generation to the next, and such copies reveal the ways in which individual readers and communities of readers used, marked, and understood their texts. From such marks and underscoring, from the highlighted or cross-hatched and even, at times, wholly obliterated pages, from pointing fingers and marked commonplaces, and especially from annotations in the margins of books, we might then begin the recovery of early modern reading, that often silent, seemingly ephemeral, and most intimate form of intellection and engagement.

Of course the annotation of reading material was not an invention of the early modern reader of books. Medieval manuscripts are covered by a repertoire of signs—punctuation, foliation, rubrics, reading accents, cross-referencing, annotation, and a variety of scribal illustrations—and these markings remind us of the continuity of habits, protocols, and attitudes toward reading over the whole of the late medieval and early modern period. Just as manuscript publication did not disappear with the advent of print, so habits of reading formed in a medieval manuscript culture had a long life in the world of print. But the powerful and regulated impulses of humanist education in the Renaissance spread the use of marginalia far beyond the professional class of medieval readers, guiding and informing the reading of a broad class of courtiers, aristocrats, and connoisseurs, of their servants and protégés, of scholars and schoolboys, and, eventually, of a wider, more socially diverse and, by the middle of the seventeenth century, of a contentious and combative field of readers.

When such early modern readers as Gabriel Harvey annotated his Tacitus,[1] or Ben Jonson marked his Martial,[2] when Lady Mary Sidney annotated Hall's *Chronicles*,[3] when Charles I marked his Shakespeare,[4] when Sir William Drake commonplaced Machiavelli,[5] and when lawyers marked their collections of statutes or members of Parliament annotated political pamphlets, they all participated in a common cultural literacy. And these are but the most obvious exemplars; the archive of marginal annotation in any of the great collections of early modern books provides a wealth of texts so marked and used. But evidence of the margin is not our only archive for this history, for the arts of reading can also be inferred from other sources and other forms of evidence: from the kinds of training readers received; from the dominant texts of the culture and the ways they were presented, distributed, and used; and from all the paratexts of early modern books—frontispieces, tables, commendatory verses, indices, plates, and, most intriguingly, those dedications and addresses in which writers, publishers, and printers at once imagined and conjured the early modern patron, reader, and marketplace for books.

The majority of early modern readers and writers of texts in classical and vernacular languages were socially and economically privileged males trained in the reading and translating of Virgil and Horace, Martial and Catullus, Juvenal and Persius. They learned to read from private tutors and in schoolrooms, and their personal and institutional experience constitutes an important source of information for reconstructing the experience of individual readers and of a significant class of consumers. They were saturated with editions of classical authors whose printed texts were surrounded by a sea of commentary. Readers and writers shared these as the common property of an education in humane letters, and in their modeling of text and commentary these editions shaped the creation and presentation of early modern literature from Spenser's *Shepheardes Calender* (1579) to Cowley's *Davideis* (1656) and from Harington's *Orlando Furioso* (1591) to Hobbes's translation of Thucydides (1629) and beyond. Printed commentary bolstered the authority of the text and guided its interpretation by situating the contemporary text and the contemporary reader in a community of learning and within a set of interpretive protocols.

Early modern reading was inflected by other models, none more important than Scripture. The English Bible was the great vernacular text whose histories, verses, epistles, and prayers supplied the steady recitative against which so many early modern literary texts were both written and read. Scripture was read in the home and from the pulpit; and sermons and homilies, paraphrases and commentaries, psalters, hymns, and prayers flowed from divines and scholars through printing presses and booksellers to readers throughout this period. Nor should we think that the paraphrasing of Latin poetry and the explication of Scripture were contradictory modes of thought or feeling. One of the great interpretive projects of the European learned community was the harmonizing of sacred and secular histories and mythologies. Indeed, the texts of Hebrew and classical antiquity were the twin foundations on which the structure of exemplary reading was based.

Habits of imitation and admiration, of application and attentiveness, were formed by parsing, translating, memorizing, and replicating both the Scriptures and the classics. These habits focused the mind on the exemplary force of the text, on what was translatable and transportable, on the 'commonplace' and the proverbial, on the didactic and moralizing, and on ethical and spiritual thematics. When Sir Philip Sidney defended poetry, it was for literature's moving and imaginative moral life; when Lady Anne Clifford consoled herself with Chaucer, it was for "his devine sperett";[6] and when Henry More recalled his father reading Spenser, he remembered a poem "richly fraught with divine morality."[7] Such modes of reverence and methods of understanding and application were echoed and reinforced by the literary, and even by the typographical, texture of vernacular literature: the adages and axioms marked for extraction, the exemplary materials set in italic type, the commonplaces marked by inverted commas, and when not literally marked, easy to discover and export. We might even think that reading was programmed by physical markers that became internalized, habitual to the act of reading, indeed to the ways in which both those who read and those who wrote imagined the work of the text. In the flourishing literature of 'sentences,' in the training to commonplace, in biblical hermeneutics and particularly in the methods of personal and national application so important to reformed traditions of reading Scripture, we find a powerful set of models for the consumption of a broad variety of texts. Manuscript commonplace books into which early modern readers transcribed miscellaneous materials—prose passages, verse extracts, poems, prayers, moral proverbs, observations—from a broad variety of their reading according to a set of abstracted categories not only provided these readers with materials for their own literary, political, and intellectual labor, but also for the advising of others, for diplomatic counsel and service, for solace and meditation, for fashioning the individual and the commonweal.

It is perfectly clear then, and from an abundance of evidence, that early modern readers turned to their books for patterns of virtue, for classical wisdom and Christian morality, for models of conduct and expression. Exemplary reading was among the most important of Renaissance intellectual techniques, and it was premised on that most ubiquitous of readerly habits, the marking and exporting of commonplaces. And yet, just as books shaped readers, so we must also acknowledge that early modern readers shaped the books they read and used. Every quotation and adaptation, every act of commonplacing and expropriation transforms the words of the author. Even more obviously, every marking and highlighting of the text transforms the book, and early modern readers, as we have seen, were assiduous markers of their texts. By hand, and often on flyleaves and endpapers, they summarized, abstracted, and indexed their books; they added pointing fingers, trefoils, lines, stars, asterisks, circles, dots, marks of engagement and 'return' to their pages; they cross-hatched the printed text, sometimes so deeply that the words became illegible; they cut and tore the pages of their books; and at times, through using and marking, through anger and disgust, they utterly obliterated the book itself. Books shaped readers, but the books that once belonged to early modern readers also bear eloquent, elaborate, and at times alarming, testimony of the ways in which readers reshaped books.

To note this variety of intellectual and physical evidence is not, however, to account for all of the complex and subtle transactions between readers and their books, and we can be certain that not all of these transactions fit straightforward models. Kevin Sharpe's recent work on Sir William Drake has given us a superb example of a perfectly conventional Stuart gentleman—the son of godly parents, a member of Parliament and a landowner, educated in modern languages and conversant with the ancients—who read not according to Renaissance norms, but against the moral and social grain, who read to construct a suspicious and amoral view of the world, who fashioned his relations in rural Buckinghamshire not according to the morality of Scripture nor in admiration of the Stoic wisdom of the ancients but according to the cynical practices of Tacitus and Machiavelli.[8] Nor does the bold contradiction of—any more than the utter compliance with—the dominant culture exhaust the possibilities of readerly attitudes; early modern readers must also have sustained a variety of complicit, resistant, and ironic relations with texts.

Surely John Donne anticipated complicity and irony when he wrote of Lucy Harington Russell, countess of Bedford (with a kind of fantastic exaggeration), that she was "God's masterpiece," "His factor for our loves," indeed "divinity" itself.[9] The bold idioms of Donne's verse epistles suggest a knowing intimacy between writer and reader, an understanding of just how far, and from what angle of ironic sophistication, theological conventions might be exploited, and how they might be read within the context of courtly compliment. The daring gestures, half-secrets, and knowing glances of these poems are staged for the sophisticated pleasure of one aristocratic patron reading from Donne's autograph; perhaps the poet also anticipated a similar if not quite so intimate reading by those few others privileged to witness—in manuscript copy, though not likely in Donne's autograph—his bold display. But what if these poems escaped the privileges of manuscript to circulate, in print, beyond the knowing few? Donne feared that migration; no doubt he wondered how those with a different sense of godliness, and reading from within a different social geography and from a text that bore no trace of the intimacies of script, would understand his handling of sacred compliment and courtly convention. And so we might ask—with nearly every text, and at every point in this, or indeed in any age—how social standing and education, how gender, age, and generation, or how godly conviction and partisan allegiance (to say nothing of irony and intellect) inflect the reading of letters and books and the uses of manuscript and print. We might also contemplate, together with the impact of changing physical forms, the different kinds of pressure that literary form itself exerts on readers: verse epistles in manuscript soliciting one range of readerly responses, the epistolary novel in print another; the scientific treatise evoking one kind of attentiveness, prophecy and astrology perhaps an allied but different kind of attention; Shakespearean tragedy in a sumptuous folio presentation provoking one set of responses, the same plays in quarto perhaps a different range of feeling.

Nor of course are such shades and gradations of readerly experience, or the articulation of intellect and feeling by literary form and physical format, particular to early modernity, or to the west. Half a century ago, the Japanese novelist Yasunari Kawabata found himself reflecting on a set of questions about reading and feeling and about the arrangements and meanings of manuscript and print that might seem to us very familiar and very contemporary indeed:

> he had always read *The Tale Of Genji* in the small type of modern editions,
> but when he came across it in a handsome old block-printed edition it made an
> entirely different impression on him. What had it been like when they read it in
> those beautiful flowing manuscripts of the age of the Heian Court? A thousand
> years ago *The Tale of Genji* was a modern novel. It could never be read that way
> again, no matter how far *Genji* studies progressed. Still, the old edition gave a
> more intense pleasure than the modern one. [10]

In one of his epistles to the countess of Bedford, Donne wrote "soon the reasons why you are loved by all grow infinite." It must seem so of the questions to be asked, of the angles to be probed, of the evidence to be sorted and weighed, of the acts of reason and depths of feeling to be imagined and reconstructed in making a history of reading. We began by wondering: Is it possible to write such history? Does evidence remain of what happened so long ago? Or of what happens now, so often, in privacy and silence? In fact the ground work has already been laid with superb studies and case histories.[11] The materials gathered for *The Reader Revealed*—the copies of annotated and rubricated books; the manuscript miscellanies, commonplace books, and diaries; the primers and hornbooks, the red-letter calendars and black-letter specimens, the chapbooks and almanacs, the pamphlets and newsbooks, the book fair and auction catalogues; the folios, quartos, and duodecimos; the Bibles, histories, and dictionaries; the dedications and addresses to readers; the architectural frontispieces and emblematic title pages, the illustrations, maps, and models—all these objects and images allow us to enter more certainly, and to imagine more deeply, the readerly past.

Kyoto, Japan

June 2001

1   These can be consulted in *Gabriel Harvey's Marginalia*, collected and edited by G. C. Moore Smith (Stratford-upon-Avon, 1913).

2   Jonson's marked copies of Martial are in the Folger Shakespeare Library: *Epigrammaton libri* (London, 1615), STC 17492 copy 1, and *M. Val. Martialis nova editio* (Leiden, 1619), PA 6501 A2 1619 Cage (cat. no. 104).

3   Folger STC 1272 copy 2.

4   See T. A. Birrell, *English Monarchs and their Books: from Henry II to Charles II* [The Panizzi Lectures, 1986] (London, 1987), 44–45.

5   See Kevin Sharpe, *Reading Revolutions: The Politics of Reading in Early Modern England* (New Haven and London, 2000), and cat. no. 12 and illustration p. 58.

6   *The Diary of Anne Clifford, 1616–1619*, ed. Katherine O. Acheson (New York, 1995), 164–5.

7   Henry More, *Philosophicall Poems* (Cambridge, 1647), sig. A2r.

8   See Sharpe, *Reading Revolutions*.

9   Quotations from Donne's verse epistles are from *John Donne*, ed. John Carey (Oxford, 1990).

10 Kawabata, *Beauty and Sadness*, trans. Howard Hibbett (New York, 1996), 34.

11 Among a number of excellent studies, see Carlo Ginzburg, *The Cheese and the Worms: The Cosmos of a Sixteenth-Century Miller* (Baltimore, MD, 1980); Robert Darnton's essays in *The Great Cat Massacre and Other Episodes in French Cultural History* (New York, 1984); Roger Chartier, *Lectures et Lecteurs dans La France d'Ancien Regime* (Paris, 1987); Anthony Grafton and Lisa Jardine, "'Studied for Action': How Gabriel Harvey Read His Livy," *Past & Present* no. 129, (1990): 30–78; William H. Sherman, *John Dee: The Politics of Reading and Writing in the English Renaissance* (Amherst, MA, 1995).

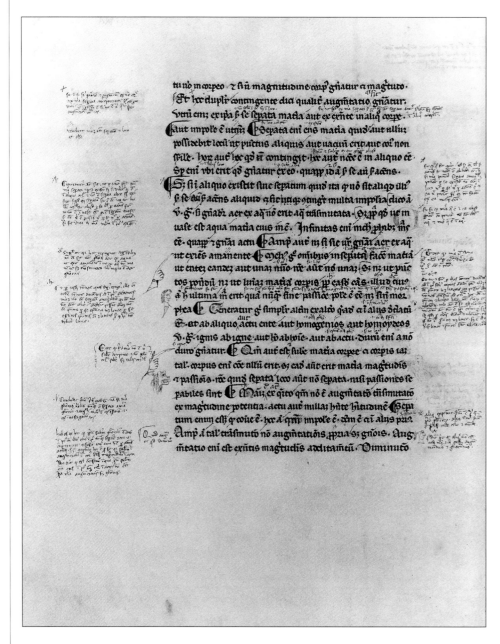

A page from Aristotle, *Physica*, Manuscript, ca. 1300 (cat. no. 69).

Red Ink and Black Letter: Reading Early Modern Authority
Sabrina Alcorn Baron

Reading and writing, from their inception, were recognized as powerful devices. Adepts who mastered them were set apart, often transcending hereditary social standing by outstripping colleagues or outsmarting superiors. A society obsessed with maintaining traditional, hierarchical order, such as early modern Europe was, viewed the transforming power of these skills with suspicion and even fear. In the early sixteenth century, the Protestant Reformation exploited reading through the new printing technology to persuade people ultimately to overturn established religious doctrines, social orders, and governments. This movement focused attention on the potential of reading to empower a populace to elude or master various social controls. The Renaissance shift from public reading in group settings to primarily solitary, silent reading, from oral to textual culture, had also exacerbated these fears. The visual and aural cues at the heart of face-to-face interaction were no longer available to guide interpretation; neither was there opportunity for in-depth discussion nor offering of multiple opinions in pursuit of meaning. In essence, printing made texts available to thousands of potential readers who were looking at texts independent of any instruction or any authority and determining meaning for themselves. This potential for the multitude to form numerous and diverse opinions on religion and politics had serious implications for the ability of church and state to maintain their traditional superior positions of power and authority in early modern society. [1]

Thus, the effects of reading needed to be limited, or at least mediated. One way to do this was to build prescriptive methods of reading into the basic appearance of text on the page. David Olson has argued that in the transition from oral to written, early readers of manuscript texts had to develop recognition of authorial intent, for example whether texts were meant to be literal or metaphorical. He describes an "interpretive gap" in the shift from one medium to another that might be bridged by "systematic, scholarly methods." [2] Laura Kendrick sees the use of illumination in medieval texts as a method of imparting the presence, and thereby, the intent of the author or the scribe or the illuminator or even God to the inanimate page because "power and authority were unimaginable without a living, enforcing presence." Paul Saenger and Michael Heinlein have discussed the evolution of annotations in incunabula as a way of influencing interpretation.[3] Establishing patterns of decoration and symbols (including words) in text was, then, a means for authors, scribes, printers, publishers, and sometimes readers to "'fix'" the text. This concept derives from Elizabeth Eisenstein's ideas about standardization of appearance and meaning that came with mechanized printing. Illuminating, rubricating, and using specific letter forms such as black letter were techniques employed earlier to fix the meaning of texts through elements of composition. Features communicating to readers the manner in which a text was intended to be read and interpreted emerged in manuscript texts, then were adapted to print until other means of limiting printed texts—like title pages, prefaces, page numbers, etc.—evolved in the new medium.[4] Early print was deliberately crafted in imitation of manuscript texts for other reasons too. Readers had become accustomed to the appearance of the scribe-produced manuscript page, so early printers maintained it in order to retain their customer base.[5] Changing the presentation of texts too radically, too quickly might have put readers off the printed text for purely aesthetic reasons, not to mention likely increasing difficulty of comprehension. Print had to work out over time a 'look' of its own that also instructed readers how to navigate and interpret texts. Conventions for limiting printed texts had to accommodate a different method of production and a different way of reading that was primarily silent and solitary, although considered as dangerous as ever, if not more so. Ultimately reader interpretation remained (and remains) uncontrollable, but it was vital for early modern cultures, which placed a premium on control and maintaining order, to make the attempt.

Red is the most compelling color in nature—the color of blood—and therefore, the most alarming color. It is also the color identified with the most powerful and uncontrollable natural force—fire.[6] Red makes humans take notice, stop, and consider what to do. For prehistoric cultures, interpretation of this symbolism often determined life or death. Recognition of red in post-industrial society echoes this primordial situation: red is used to control one of the deadliest forces on the planet—the flow of automobile traffic. It is not surprising then that red is the color that communicates power. Moreover, red has been fundamental to graphic expression since prehistoric times, when red pigment was derived from blood. Later other pigments (red ochre, or rubric) imparted the same hues.[7] Ancient libraries often had names and other information written on their walls in red, and the use of red ink for emphasis in writing originated with the ancient Egyptians.[8] Thus red has been fundamental in historic human understanding, graphic expression, and organization of knowledge almost from the beginning.

The color red was a natural choice for representing authority on paper. It directed the reader's response to the situation at hand: controlling interaction with and interpretation of the text. In the eleventh and twelfth centuries, when England was making the transition from reliance on orally transmitted memories to reliance on written records, a number of symbols evolved as signposts to help readers determine what Walter J. Ong has called the "visual location of materials in a manuscript text."[9] The symbols included larger, decorated initial capitals; underlining; paragraph marks; page and section headings; foliation or page numbering; red ruling in the margins and around the text; and connecting lines, brackets, manicules (pointing hands) and other symbols linking the text with marginal glosses, commentary, or annotation. Naturally, the force of red ink was lent to these textual guides as they developed.[10] One of the clearest examples of the relationship between authority and textual expression is found in legal documents and texts. A manuscript volume in the Folger Shakespeare Library catalogued as "A collection of statutes of the realm, c.1225–c.1309" (cat. no. 15) has stereotypical red decorated initials at the beginning of different sections of the text. The documents are also rubricated with red and blue paragraph marks, punctuation, and have important pieces of information, such as sums of money, introduced with red markings.

Such red instructions continued to be applied to early printed books by hand and were occasionally printed on the page by a press. Johann Gutenberg set headings in red for five pages of the 42-line Bible (cat. no. 112), evidence that red and black could be printed beautifully and with ease on the same type form from the beginning. But Gutenberg resorted to red and blue hand-rubrication for the bulk of the work as did most other early printers. Curt Bühler suggests that little red printing was done in the earliest years of hand-press printing because of a battle over commercial turf between established illuminators and emerging printers, while others have argued that hand rubrication endured because red printing was too costly.[11] The illuminator was presented as integral to book production in Jost Amman's trade scenes (cat. no. 7), originally published in 1568, although the commercial application of red ink by hand disappeared from printed books "sometime in the early to mid-sixteenth century."[12]

Red ink was used also in readers' manuscript annotation of printed texts. One example is Richard Stonley, a sixteenth-century English Exchequer official, who recorded in his diary regular purchases of red ink along with other writing supplies.[13] Another example is in Folger copy 4 of Samuel Daniel's *The collection of the historie of England* (1626) (cat. no. 20) where a reader has underlined the names of kings in red ink, the manner in which proper names were identified in manuscript texts before more systematic capitalization developed. A reader also drew symbols and wrote the Latin word "*NOTA*" in red in the margins to direct attention to sections of the printed text. Readers' marginalia and notes in a Folger copy of Littleton's *TENVRES* (cat. no. 48) are written in red ink in conjunction with black. John White advised in *A rich cabinet* (1668) (cat. no. 34), a book of helpful hints, that those learning to read from a printed text would benefit from having a red dot placed under the syllables of words. Locating red dots under syllables of words was a medieval method of placing emphasis.[14] Manuscript scribes frequently ruled margins in red, establishing boundaries, or limits, for the block of text written on the page. One of the many examples in the Folger collection is the volume of epigrams written by Sir John Harington for Prince Henry in 1605 (cat. no. 71). The beautiful italic script is kept firmly in check by red lines establishing the margin. Early modern adaptations of margins ruled in red by readers can be found in printed texts, for example, in the Folger copy of

Francis Bacon's *De sapientia veterum liber* (1634) (cat. no. 19). A reader has constructed a margin-within-the-margin by enclosing the blank space left and right of the text block in red ink. Inside these red-ruled spaces, the reader has transliterated the text, or notes on the text, into shorthand, which was just becoming popular in the 1630s. The traditional authority of red-ruled margins validated the novelty of shorthand in a text addressing the wisdom of the ancients. Another instance of red ruling to lend authority to text is in the Folger volumes of royal proclamations assembled by Humphrey Dyson, the Jacobean collector of ephemera (cat. no. 14). To reinforce perceptions of authority, Dyson drew red-ruled margins and underlined sections of the black-letter text of Queen Elizabeth I's instructions to her people.[15] These examples suggest some larger cultural retention of medieval annotating practices had endured among early modern English readers. They also testify to the abiding recognition of red ink as signifying importance.

As red ink applied to printed texts in production by hand disappeared, this application was adapted more and more to the printing press. The early Venetian printer Erhard Ratdolt printed red ornaments and page borders in his highly decorated books.[16] Lawrence Andrewe's 1527 reprint of *The myrrour[and]descrypcon of the worlde* had the first two words of the title printed in large red letters on the title page (cat. no. 31). Paragraph marks indicating where various divisions and subdivisions of text begin and other signposts in red could be easily integrated into print as they were in Miles Coverdale's English translation of the New Testament (cat. no. 16). Its running heads, rulings around the text, titles, initial capitals, manicules, asterisks, Maltese crosses, double dashes, and marginal cross references to Old Testament passages were printed in red.

It was in liturgical texts in fact that red printing reached its zenith. In printed liturgical texts, as in their manuscript predecessors, instructions for the priest conducting church services were printed in red. This practice is illustrated by the 1554 *Manuale*, a service book used by priests, printed in England (cat. no. 18). Such a book naturally included lots of instructions, so large sections of the text, as well as elements of the musical notation, are in red, to the extent that red dominates the page and the black-letter print fades into insignificance. Rubrication marks traditionally rendered in red are in this *Manuale* often supplied in black to provide sufficient contrast. The Roman Catholic primer, a book designed for use in private devotions, also had instructions printed in red. In addition, the important words of the title in a Rouen edition of 1555 (cat. no. 17)—*Prymer*, *Englyshhe*, and *Saru[m]*— are in red, as are running heads and large initial capitals. The Kalendar at the front of the book used red ink to highlight particularly important holy days such as Easter and Christmas, the origin of a familiar adage: 'red-letter day.' When the Kalendar was adapted for use in more secular almanacs, red ink contrasted with black was retained. *Rider's British Merlin*, a popular late-seventeenth-century almanac, had not only a calendar in red and black, but also had important words on the title page, like *Leap-Year*, in red (cat. no. 13).

Printed uses of red ink continued to crop up occasionally outside liturgical texts, and such secular use increased over the course of the seventeenth century. In Clement Walker's *Anarchia Anglicana* (1649) (cat. no. 21), for example, red delineates the names of those men who had signed Charles I's death warrant—the regicides.[17] Here red ink is a direct substitute for blood. It portrays the power and authority vested in royal blood by early modern societies. From the mid-seventeenth century the presence of red ink on the title page was greatly expanded. Walker's pro-royalist work discussed above featured a red and black title page as did the first edition of John Milton's anti-royalist diatribe, *EIKONOKLASTES* (Mathew Simmons, 1649). Both sides in the debate on monarchy tried to appropriate to their cause the power and authority of blood represented by red ink. A luxurious foray into subscription publishing in the 1650s, John Ogilby's lavishly illustrated edition of Virgil's works, featured red print on the title page (cat. no. 44). Once again, red was chosen to highlight the most important words, such as the author's name, features of the book, and the author's address where the book was for sale. Printers and publishers were quick to capitalize on red ink's power to attract readers and buyers.

'Black letter' describes most medieval script—writing "in which the darkness of the letters overpowers the whiteness of the page."[18] The forms that evolved in Northern Europe were more angular and pointed in appearance, or "condensed," and became associated with vernacular texts while those in Southern Europe were more rounded and used less in common texts. Black letter evolved to facilitate ligatures, long words, and diphthongs. It better accommodated abbreviations and was more space-efficient overall, working well in the double-column page layout. The script was also believed to be conducive to "continuous reading."[19]

When Gutenberg was designing and cutting the first multiple-character metal type in the mid-fifteenth century, he modeled it on the script most familiar to him. In fact, since he was planning to print the Bible, he modeled it on the script most familiar to him from liturgical texts, a variation of black letter known as textura.[20] Its compatibility with two-column layout and facility with abbreviations is striking in the 42-line Bible. The second printer to operate in England, Wynkyn de Worde, used a French-cut, black-letter type around the turn of the sixteenth century, but rather quickly thereafter black letter began to fade as the dominant European type due to the increased use of roman and italic fonts popularized by the Italian Renaissance and humanism. These movements fostered a tendency to render the revived texts of antiquity in a script, and subsequently type, that closely resembled Roman carved inscriptions. Roman type became dominant in Europe primarily through the printing of the influential and prolific Venetian printer, Aldus Manutius. His designs affected Italian types most directly but also had a significant pan-European effect.

Roman type was introduced into English printing around 1508 and italic followed a couple of decades later in the work of de Worde.[21] In the Elizabethan era, English printing, which always lagged behind that on the Continent, continued to be for the most part in black letter, although roman was becoming more popular. Economics played a role here too; English printers used what type they had, and that was black letter. No type founders were working in England prior to the 1560s, necessitating expensive importation of type from the Continent. Subsequently, the shift to roman type in other areas of Europe made black letter cheaper and easier to acquire. So for reasons of economy and convenience, English printers held on to, and continued to use, their black letter as it was supplanted on the Continent. Black letter dominance in England was over, however, by the 1630s. Stanley Morison pointed out a gradual change over time as the result of a combination of factors, perhaps most importantly the growth of the reading public, in which more and better educated readers identified with roman type.[22]

The printing history of the most widely printed—and read—text in early modern England, the Bible, provides a microcosm of the general shift from black letter to roman. In the 1530s Coverdale's New Testament, the first allowed English translation, was printed on the Continent in black letter, as was the Great Bible, the English translation authorized by Henry VIII to supplant Coverdale in 1539. The Great Bible was the prototype for all English translations until the so-called Geneva Bible appeared in 1560, also translated and printed abroad, and printed in roman type according to Continental conventions. (It also numbered the verses instead of using red-ink rubrication marks to provide readers' cues.) But when this version with extensive marginal notes, glosses, and cross-references came to be viewed as problematic because it promoted diversity of opinion in religion, the Elizabethan church countered with its own, more conservative translation, the Bishops' Bible, printed in black letter in 1568.[23] The new, and allegedly improved, translation sponsored by King James I was printed in 1611 as a black-letter folio. Yet this edition was expensive and unwieldy, and moreover, due to popularity of the Geneva Bible, a large body of Anglo-Scots readers were accustomed to reading the Bible in roman type. In 1612–13 a more manageable roman quarto edition of the King James version was issued, followed by a roman octavo version in 1613.[24] Roman type was now considered acceptable for printing the Bible and the English reading public was growing accustomed to it over time, despite the persistence of black letter for a variety of reasons, including insularity and economics.

In England a more specialized application of black letter endured. The type had become identified with 'common' vernacular texts designed for "circles untouched by humanistic studies" and was often identified as "English" type. This identification is evidenced in the 1632 edition of Jacob Cats's polyglot emblem book, *Spiegel van den ouden ende nieuwen tijdt* (cat. no. 50), where English words were printed in black letter, but other type was employed for other languages. A glossary of words appended to Edmund Coote's *The English school-master* (1670) (cat. no. 77), entitled "Directions for the unskilful," explains that different languages are identified by the type in which they are set: roman for Latin and "other learned Languages"; italic for French words that had come into English; and "those with the English letter are meerley English, or from some other vulgar tongue."[25] Familiarity, if not physiology, made black letter easier to read and comprehend, and it was therefore ideal for reaching a wide reading audience. Black letter represented historical writing and printing practice, and so the power and authority of tradition. For these reasons, as well as other cultural tendencies noted above, black letter survived in the seventeenth century as the dominant font in specific categories of texts at the exact same time it was declining in others. It survived in some editions of the Bible,[26] in prayer books, primers, ABCs, hornbooks, early chapbooks, law books,[27] published laws, and statutes—texts issued in the voice of authority, whether divine or civil; texts which instilled obedience, singularity of opinion, and uniformity of action.

Effectively conveying the authority necessary for the church and state to maintain control over society required accessibility and pointed interpretive guidance at all levels of society and at all levels of literacy.[28] Black letter, the type used for hornbooks and other reading manuals, was the type that beginning English readers encountered first. With study, repetition, and memorization, it became the most familiar. The preference for black letter in teaching reading is evident in a brief survey of sample titles in the Folger collection. Both hornbooks and the primers, derived from the Roman Catholic books of devotion discussed above, were essential in early modern childhood education and were printed in black letter. Here again, in the religious texts that constituted the hornbooks and primers, black-letter type was employed in an authoritative manner, functioning on two levels to teach reading and obedience together. Obedience to God and his church encompassed and reinforced obedience to God's chosen monarch at the head of the early modern state.[29]

Richard Tottell, at the end of his preface to the seventh edition of his bestselling verse miscellany printed in black letter, exhorted "the unlearned, by readinge to learne to bee more skilfull…" (cat. no. 39). In the late sixteenth century, John Hart advocated spelling reform in England in imitation of contemporary movements on the more progressive Continent. He argued for reform on the grounds that letters and sounds had been misrepresented historically, making reading English more difficult than it needed to be and thus inhibiting literacy. Hart made this argument in a publication that presented text for the student reader in the traditional black letter.[30] *Most easie instructions for reading*, a slight pamphlet dated to 1610 and intended for adults learning to read, was printed in black letter except for the instructions to the teacher, which were in roman (cat. no. 26). A century after Hart, the thirty-sixth edition of Edmund Coote's highly favored reading and writing textbook, designed for teaching tradesmen's apprentices or small children, followed the same pattern—roman for the teacher, black letter for the student (cat. no. 77). The first two sections of the book, where most of the black-letter type occurs, could be separated from the rest for teaching the least skilled students, who might damage or destroy it. Coote's preface points out that the first two pages of his text, containing the alphabet, syllables, and the Lord's Prayer in black letter, had been adopted by his printer for use in hornbooks.[31]

English readers with brief, or superficial education, who consequently attained only rudimentary levels of reading literacy often had access only to black letter. If black letter transmitted the voice of authority, it was primarily received by the eyes and minds of the least literate, least sophisticated readers. Keith Thomas characterized black letter as "the type for the common people," and pointed out "black-letter literacy" as "a more basic skill than roman-type literacy."[32] A collection of late-seventeenth-century chapbooks in the Folger bears this out (cat. no. 43). These humble little books sold for two pence each and were intended to instruct readers in morals and citizenship. Torn, soiled, and misshapen from use, they had crude woodcut illustrations on their title pages to attract the rudimentary reader's attention and black-letter text inside to hold it. Many people could "read anything that is Printed indifferently," but did not have the ability to read script.[33] They were familiar with the black letter of the hornbook and primer, reflections of secretary script, the most common English script in the sixteenth and seventeenth centuries, but not the more cosmo-politan italic handwriting promoted by humanism.

Specialized use of black letter reinforced its associations with authoritarian controls. Just as fundamental religious precepts were printed in black letter, so was the essential will of the state in legal documents and texts. Sir Edward Littleton's late-medieval explication of English land tenures, an essential law text for centuries, was printed in black letter (cat. no. 48). The 1586 edition printed by Richard Tottell, the foremost English producer of law books in the sixteenth century, had roman and italic type on the title page, running heads and Latin quotes in roman, but the body of the text in black letter. Tottell printed the verse miscellany mentioned above in black letter because that was the type he obtained from Richard Grafton, and that was the type he used to print the law books in which he specialized. A printed collection of acts passed in the Parliament of 1543, including an act decreeing who might read the Bible aloud to others in public and who could read the Bible only silently to themselves, appeared in black letter (cat. no. 62), as did the edition of Jacobean and early Caroline statutes printed in 1624, apparently intended for the use of lawyers and legal officials (cat. no. 97). Royal proclamations over the course of the seventeenth century also continued to be printed in black letter. Transmitting the voice of the king and the force of his government, intended to be as strong and binding as that of parliamentary statutes, procla-mations often addressed immediate emergencies, such as the apprehension of criminals, or the recall and destruction of seditious books, and were directed at the widest possible audience, to be interpreted in the gravest manner.

Black letter continues to be used occasionally in post-modern society. Moreover, when it is used, it still conveys power and authority in print. Consider, for example, the mastheads of the most authoritative and august print news publications—including *The New York Times*, *The Washington Post*, and *The Chicago Tribune*. Newspapers use the top half of the front page to emphasize the most important news stories that will appeal to readers. The appearance of this area thus needs to stand out, to impress readers and reinforce the authority of the information in the stories 'above the fold.' *The New York Times* with its black-letter masthead carries more authority than *USA Today*, or so the printers and publishers of *The Times* would have us believe. Black letter sends a particular message, guiding readers to particular interpretations of news stories.

First employed as visually appealing decoration, red ink and black letter doubled as practical devices for guiding the reader through texts. Symbols provided in red ink and symbolism infused in black-letter type informed the reader how a text should be read and interpreted. As print developed its own conventions for these purposes, such as prefaces addressed "To the Reader," manuscript conventions began to disappear. The preface "To the Reader" in Richard Tottell's mid-sixteenth-century verse miscellany was, for example, widely imitated (cat. no. 39). Over the course of the seventeenth century, books with multiple addresses to the reader treating issues ranging from printer's errors to the cosmic significance of the preface itself, such as Lily's *Grammar* (cat. no. 75), the First Folio of Shakespeare's collected works (cat. nos. 32 and 76), and Humphrey Moseley's collection of William Cartwright's works (cat. no. 78), became common. Some books had addresses to the reader at the beginning, in the middle (cat. no. 75), and at the end of the text (cat. no. 77). By the end of the seventeenth century, books without prefaces were "indifferently" received, "as a Minister without his Credentials." "Custom" had "obliged every Author to give some account of his Labour before he can hope to engage any Body to try its Worth."[34] A 'canonical' spatial arrangement of the elements of a printed book, as well as the layout of the individual pages, also developed to guide and instruct readers, but the preface was the most direct way to shape readers' interactions with, and interpretations of, texts.

The authority of the natural forces embodied by red recommended it to other authoritative uses in church and state. As a dye or pigment, the scarlet shades of red were expensive, and so available only to the higher orders of society wealthy enough to afford them. Red was thus identified with the power and stature of aristocratic wealth, social status, political power, and royal rank. In the Roman Catholic Church, it was the color reserved to cardinals, the princes of the Church at the top of the hierarchy. Red ink in a text provided direction and instruction: text in red to instruct the priest and text in black for the common worshiper.

This color coding assisted readers in navigating texts, leading them to a particular interpretation. Black letter was identified as stereotypically 'English,' the script, or type, of the common people. It was used to print vernacular texts, primarily issued by the crown as head of the state and head of the church, texts promulgated in support of authoritarian offices and institutions. Known from traditional and common use, red ink and black letter presented familiar patterns and provoked familiar responses in even the least literate readers. They both effected and affected reading practices, allowing readers to traverse the physical terrain of the written and printed text while at the same time guiding readers to responses desirable to church and state. The use of textual features created as well as controlled reading practices, working to diffuse, or at least temper, fears that civil and religious authorities harbored about reading, especially the silent, solitary reading prevalent from the Renaissance forward.

1   This discussion was influenced by Alberto Manguel, *A History of Reading* (New York, 1996); David R. Olson, *The World on Paper: The Conceptual and Cognitive Implications of Writing and Reading* (Cambridge, 1994); and Walter J. Ong, *Orality and Literacy: The Technologizing of the Word* (London and New York, 1982). See also M. B. Parkes, *Pause and Effect: An Introduction to the History of Punctuation in the West* (Berkeley and Los Angeles, CA, 1993), and Laura Kendrick, *Animating the Letter: The Figurative Embodiment of Writing from Late Antiquity to the Renaissance* (Columbus, OH, 1999).

2   Olson, 57, 187, 190, 193–94, 260–61. See also J. P. Gumbert, "'Typography' in the Manuscript Book," *Journal of the Printing Historical Society* 22 (1993): 5–28.

3   Kendrick, 21, 24; Olson, 261; Gumbert, 7. Erasmus was very concerned about and personally involved in the punctuation of his work because he believed it governed interpretation. Paul Saenger and Michael Heinlein, "Incunable Description and Its Implication for the Analysis of Fifteenth-Century Reading Habits," in *Printing the Written Word: The Social History of Books, circa 1450–1520*, Sandra Hindman ed. (Ithaca, NY, 1991), 255–56.

4   Elizabeth L. Eisenstein, *The Printing Press as an Agent of Change*, 2 vols. (Cambridge, 1979; repr. 1997); Kendrick, 178.

5   S. H. Steinberg, *Five Hundred Years of Printing*, rev. ed., ed. John Trevitt (Newcastle, DE, 1996), 10; Gumbert, 6.

6   *Oxford English Dictionary Online* (Oxford, 2000), s.v. "red;" David N. Carvalho, *Forty Centuries of Ink* (New York, 1904), 4.

7   *OED*; Kendrick, 15.

8   Gumbert, 12–13; Saenger and Heinlein, 250–51. I am grateful to Eleanor Shevlyn for discussion on these points.

9   Ong, 124–25; Keith Thomas, "The Meaning of Literacy in Early Modern England," in *The Written Word: Literacy in Tradition*, Gerd Baumann ed. (Oxford, 1986), 98.

10 Isa Fleischmann-Heck, "Script in Practical Use: Reading and Writing in the Late Middle Ages," in *Gutenberg Man of the Millennium: From a secret enterprise to the first media revolution* (Mainz, 2000), 86–87; Margaret E. Smith, "Patterns of Incomplete Rubrication in Incunables and what they suggest about working methods," in *Medieval Book Production: Assessing the Evidence*, Linda Brownrigg ed. (Los Altos Hills, CA, 1990), 133–34 (I am grateful to Kathleen Lynch for this reference.); Saenger and Heinlein, 243–49.

11 Eva-Maria Hanebutt-Benz, "Gutenberg's Inventions: The Technical Aspects of Printing with Multiple Letters on the Letterpress Printing Machine," in *Gutenberg Man of the Millennium*, 118–19; "Catalogue," ibid., 181; Curt F. Bühler, *The Fifteenth-Century Book: The Scribes. The Printers. The Decorators.* (Philadelphia, PA, 1960), 71–72, 74, 163; Saenger and Heinlein, 251–52.

12 Smith, 133, 141; Jost Amman and Hans Sachs, *The Book of Trades (Standebuch)*, introduction by Benjamin A. Rifkin (New York, 1973), ix.

13 Gumbert, 12–13.

14 I am grateful to Susan Scola for pointing out this passage.

15 William A. Jackson, "Humphrey Dyson and His Collections of Elizabethan Proclamations," *Harvard Library Bulletin* 1 (1947): 76–89. I am grateful to Sullen Towers for this reference.

16 Charles Thomas-Stanford, *Early Editions of Euclid's Elements* (London, 1926), 1.

17 The red printing appears in two copies held by the Folger.

18 Carvalho, 91; Peter Bain and Paul Shaw, "Blackletter: Type and National Identity," *Printing History* 38/39 (1999): 4.

19 Stanley Morison, *Politics and Script: Aspects of Authority and Freedom in the Development of Politics and Script from the Sixth Century B. C. to the Twentieth Century A. D.* (Oxford, 1972), 235; "Black Letter: its Origin and Current Use," *The Monotype Recorder* 36 (1937): 7–10, 12; Geoffrey Dowding, *An Introduction to the History of Printing Types* (London, 1961), 5, 7.

20 Bain and Shaw, 4, 8; Steinberg, 9; Hanebutt-Benz, 98.

21 [Morison], "Black Letter," 9; Steinberg, 11.

22 W. Craig Ferguson, *Pica Roman Type in Elizabethan England* (Aldershot, 1989); Steinberg, 82; [Morison], "Black Letter," 9; M. H. Black, "The Printed Bible," in *The Cambridge History of the Bible, Volume 2: The West from the Reformation to the Present Day*, S. L. Greenslade ed. (Cambridge, 1963), 163. I am grateful to Peter Blayney for discussions on this topic.

23 Stanley Morison, *English Prayer Books* (Cambridge, 1949), 53, 110–11, 114; Black, 444.

24 Black, 454–55.

25 [Morison], "Black Letter," 11–12; Bain and Shaw, 38; Coote, 58. "English" in both instances in Coote's comment is set in black letter.

26 Black letter may have endured in Bibles due to its facility in the two-column layout and because it was more economical in terms of space, leading to a small printed volume. Black, 426–27, 436.

27 Ferguson, 31–32.

28 I am grateful to Richard Tuck for discussion on these points.

29 Morison, *English Prayer Books*, 67–68.

30 The following passage from Hart's table of contents: "Then followeth the newe maner of teaching, whereby who so can read English onely, may alone learne the order following, and so bee able to teach the same to others that knowe no letter, to read thereafter in a very short time" begs the question of what Hart referred to when he said "English." In this context, he may have meant black-letter type rather than the language.

31   Coote, sig. A3r.

32   Thomas, 99; Charles Mish, "Black Letter as a Social Discriminant in the Seventeenth Century," *Publications of the Modern Language Association* 68 (1953): 627–30.

33   *G. D.'s DIRECTIONS FOR WRITING . . . A. D. 1656* (Cambridge, 1933), 6.

34   Cockburn, cat. no. 75, sig. A2r.

John Dee Reads Books of Magic
Anthony Grafton

"Note this, 1567." With this laconic marginal note John Dee called attention to a striking comment about demons which he had come across in a work Ascribed to the eleventh-century Byzantine scholar Michael Psellus. "Even if demons promise us wealth and glory," Psellus had written, "they can still give us nothing on their own, for they have no power."[1] Dee's interest in this passage seems typical of the man. So does the book as a whole—a collection of late antique, medieval, and modern texts by, among others, the legendary Egyptian sage Hermes Trismegistus and the modern Florentine astrologer and medical man, Marsilio Ficino, dealing with the mysteries of the ancient Near East, the interpretation of dreams, and the best forms of therapy for the scholar threatened by the malevolent influence of Saturn. Dee is best remembered, after all, as a magus who regularly tried to speak with supernatural beings. For many years, first in England and then on the Continent, Dee held indirect conversations with angels, who offered him revelations of many kinds about their language, the structure of the universe, and the future of humanity. He and his scryers—Edward Kelly and the others who actually saw, or claimed to see, the angels appear—recorded these dialogues in elaborate diaries. Dee—and at least some of his patrons—saw these as the records of his most remarkable accomplishments, though they would later be used, in the sober age of the New Philosophy, to discredit him as an "enthusiast."[2]

Dee certainly was a magus, as Frances Yates and others have shown.[3] He dedicated himself to the study of natural magic and related fields like astrology and alchemy. He steeped himself in standard works like the Renaissance magician's dangerous but indispensable desk reference, Henry Cornelius Agrippa's *De occulta philosophia* (1533), as well as a vast range of other sources, Islamic and Jewish, ancient, medieval, and modern. His works included one of the most suggestive Renaissance texts on magic, the *Monas hieroglyphica*. And his activities included such standard ones, for Renaissance magicians, as the creation of automata. At Cambridge in 1547, he not only staged a production of Aristophanes' *Pax* at Trinity College, but also devised a "machine" for it "with the performance of the Scarabaeus, his flying up to Jupiter's palace, with a man and his basket of victuals on her back: whereat was great wondering, and many vain reports spread abroad of the means how it was effected."[4]

But Dee's pursuits ranged far more widely than general terms like 'magus' might suggest. His conversations with angels, as Deborah Harkness has shown, did not cover the standard topics of natural or demonic magic, as normally practiced in the sixteenth century. And the pursuits that won him extensive patronage from the English court included not only the astrological skills that qualified him to fix the date and time of Elizabeth's coronation, but also a wide range of mathematical and historical studies that enabled him to offer

John Dee's signature in Marsilio Ficino, *De triplici vita*, Venice, 1516 (cat. no. 110).

valued advice on calendar reform, cartography, and the expansion of the English empire. Dee studied and worked extensively on the Continent. He knew eminent mathematicians and cartographers like Oronce Fine and Gerardus Mercator, collected and studied globes and astronomical instruments, and collaborated with Henry Billingsley to produce the first English edition of Euclid in 1570. The magus who spoke with angels also corresponded with mathematicians, engineers, and Privy Councillors.

For all their diversity, Dee's activities rested on at least one common pursuit: reading. From early in his career, Dee was a passionate reader. He learned reading as a formal art in one of the great centers of English humanism, St. John's College, Cambridge, where he studied with John Cheke. The skills he mastered there won him recognition as early as 1546, when he was elected fellow and underreader in Greek at the brand-new Trinity College. He used a Europe-wide network of connections with friends and dealers to build up the largest private library in Renaissance England—one richer in the literature of such fields as Hebrew and astronomy than any institutional collection of the time.[5] And he spun rich webs of marginalia to fill the empty spaces of his books, turning each of them into something highly personal. Dee's books metamorphosized into memory palaces which recorded his experiences, components of a massive reference apparatus that he could consult with ease and efficiency, and records of a life-long conversation with writers ancient and modern. In an age when learned readers were in demand as teachers, counselors, and masters of the courtly life, Dee was the high lord of manuscript and print.[6] The anthology of esoterica, which Dee seems to have bought and read in the 1560s, and which is now in the Folger Shakespeare Library, richly documents his practices as a reader (cat. no. 110).

Humanists learned when young to personalize their books. Signatures and dates identified printed books as the property of an individual. Gabriel Harvey, one of the most systematic and thorough readers in sixteenth-century England, regularly equipped his books not only with signatures, but with mottos like "By art and labor" and with professions that his library really belonged not to him alone, but to "Gabriel Harvey and his friends."[7] Dee signed his anthology of works on magic and related subjects on the title page, but he did not add the date of acquisition—as he did in 1568, for example, to his copy of Paulus Crusius's work on the motion of the sun, now in the British Library.[8]

The identification of a humanist's book meant more than simply a record of ownership, designed to instill shame in borrowers who forgot to return a friend's treasures. Harvey and others made their books into records of the social circles they inhabited, using title pages, margins, and blank leaves to give detailed accounts of remarkable experiences and conversations. Annotated books regularly turned into something between diaries and historical records, efforts to freeze and preserve for posterity the talk and buzz of a particular intellectual world.

Dee, who kept regular diaries, did not confide in his books as often as some other scholars did. But in this case, at least one passage provoked him to add a fascinating autobiographical record. Ficino, in his encyclopedic treatise *De vita*, discussed a gem he had seen "at Florence, brought from India, where it had been dug from the head of a dragon. It was round, in the form of a coin, and naturally and neatly decorated with a great many points, which were rather like stars. When vinegar was poured on it moved in a circle, until the vapor of the vinegar dispersed."[9] In a marginal note to this passage, Dee recalled how he had studied a similar specimen in distinguished company some years before: "I saw a stone like this one, and of the same quality, in 1552 or 1553. Present were Cardano of Milan, John Francis [Offusius], and Monsieur Braudaulphin, the ambassador of the French king, in the ambassador's house at Southwark."[10] This short but vivid note makes clear how magical pursuits and political ambitions could go together in Dee's world.

For the most part, naturally, Dee read less in order to supplement his books than to learn from them. Scholarly readers deployed many forms of annotation in order to manage the vast amount of information their favorite texts contained.[11] The Ferrarese humanist Celio Calcagnini, for example, described the widespread practice of using "little towers, point hands, and little columns" to serve as aids to memory—only to reject it.[12] But even he made a habit, as he remarked, both of copying passages into notebooks and of "giving a separate summary, in the margin, of everything at all worthy of note." By doing so, he found, he could go back through "many volumes in half an hour."[13]

Dee, like Calcagnini, not only personalized his book, but transformed it into a carefully organized work of reference. He underlined many words and phrases. He drew vertical lines by especially significant passages. He noted parallels, to others' works and to his own. And he used single words and pithy phrases to single out and summarize passages that he found especially notable. One of the most challenging texts in his collection was the *Asclepius*—a dialogue in Latin on the secrets of Egyptian theology and philosophy, probably based on a lost Greek original, and traditionally, but wrongly, ascribed to the ancient writer Apuleius.[14] In the course of this work, Trismegistus described Egypt in a passionate, eloquent passage as "an image of heaven." He tragically evoked the days to come, when "The land that was the seat of reverence will be widowed by the powers and left destitute of their presence." "Then," he cried,

> this most holy land, seat of shrines and temples, will be filled completely with
> tombs and corpses. O Egypt, Egypt, of your reverent deeds only stories will survive,
> and they will be incredible to your children! Only words cut in stone will survive
> to tell your faithful works, and the Scythian or Indian or some such neighbor
> barbarian will dwell in Egypt. For divinity goes back to heaven, and all the people
> will die, deserted, as Egypt will be widowed and deserted by god and human.[15]

"Such," Trismegistus went on to say, "will be the old age of the world." But he added encouraging remarks, explaining that God would finally punish these crimes and restore the world, which after all "is his image—good from good."[16]

Dee peppered the margins of this passage with words and phrases pulled from it to form a running summary of the whole:

Prophecy.

Pyramids of Mercury, with hieroglyphics.

Old age of the world.

The flood or conflagration of the universe.

The reformation of the world.

The world is the image of god.

This blow-by-blow synopsis suggests how striking Dee found the passage—as did many other readers in the sixteenth and seventeenth centuries.[17]

But Dee's notes suggest something more as well. Well-trained humanists did not simply note down the surface meanings of their texts. They also interpreted as they read, looking for correspondences with other works, ancient and modern, identifying sources, and working out larger patterns of authorial intention that might lurk behind a deliberately obscure passage.[18] Dee, in reading the *Asclepius*, seems to have been struck especially by the eschatological character of this passage—its apparent confirmation of Old and New Testament prophecies about the end of the world. Many medieval and early modern readers took such correspondences between the Hermetica and the Bible as evidence that the Egyptians had benefited from a partial revelation of the truth—perhaps granted by God, perhaps by the devil. These parallels played a central role in the interpretations of the Hermetic texts devised by Ficino and later Christian Hermetists.[19] At least one further annotation confirms that Dee too found evidences of Jewish and Christian doctrines in these largely pagan texts. Hermes, in one of the texts in Dee's collection, describes God as crying out "with a holy word, expand, grow up, propagate all my seeds and works." "Be fruitful and multiply," wrote Dee in the margin, noting the parallel to Genesis 1:22.

Humanists, of course, often read their texts with a critical eye, looking for bibliographical and biographical information about their authors and trying to assess the quality of their texts—the same sorts of information that Dee and others recorded in some of their marginal notes.[20] Trained as Dee was in the most up-to-date scholarly techniques, he adopted this practice as well. His copy of the thirteenth-century work on magnetism by Petrus Peregrinus, which he bought in 1562, is now in the British Library.

Its margins show numerous efforts to establish the author's dates, bibliography, and reputation.[21] Dee's Folger text shows him noting Jamblichus's reference to "the books of Mercury"—at least a modest effort to clarify the shadowy history of the Hermetic books that meant so much to him.[22]

More remarkable are the notes in which Dee glossed Ficino's free Latin rendering of Synesius's work on the interpretation of dreams. This student of the Alexandrian philosopher Hypatia, who later became a Christian bishop, found avid readers in the sixteenth- and seventeenth-century heyday of dream interpretation. Dee wrote in the original Greek of certain passages beside Ficino's Latin. And at least once he vigorously criticized Ficino for omitting a word from the original "even though it is of great importance, and in the next chapter he begins from it again."[23] Frances Yates argued, in her great book on Giordano Bruno and the Hermetic tradition, that the humanistic and magical traditions were basically opposed to one another. Philologists like Erasmus distrusted the easy syncretism that found parallels to the Bible in texts by ancient Egyptian magi. Dee's case makes, at the least, a formidable exception to this rule. Evidently he felt no discomfort at all when he applied the most up-to-date tools of humanistic scholarship to the magical works of late antiquity.

The personal and the methodical often came together in the margins of a scholar's book—especially when he tried to make a particular text confirm or extend his own theories, and those of his contemporaries. Dee was quite taken with Synesius's treatment of dreams. He noted that he had made very similar arguments, before he knew the text: "I wrote in the same way," he wrote by a passage on the harmony of the universe, "and by no means did I grasp the point by reading this."[24] Synesius's version of the metaphor of the book of nature struck even more chords. "If all things are signified by all things," Synesius wrote, "since all things are related in the single creature which is the world, and these things resemble letters of all forms, signed in the world as in a book," the wise man will be able to decipher the world's message. Dee pointed out the similarity of this passage to Paracelsus's influential doctrine of signatures. And he noted that Synesius also seemed to describe "my own Cabala of being"—the secret doctrine of nature that the angels revealed to Dee in its fullest form.[25]

Dee's practices as a reader reveal much. They make clear that he continued to apply, throughout his life, the basic skills that he had mastered as a young student in grammar school and at Cambridge. They show that he—like Agrippa and a number of other natural magicians—saw no contradiction between the pursuit of precise philological knowledge about the ancients and the belief that ancient texts might provide essential secrets about God and the cosmos, revealed thousands of years before to Egyptian sages. And they confirm that any full biography of Dee—or of many other, similar figures—will have to take full account not only of the texts he published and the letters he wrote, but also of the archipelago of summaries, reflections, and debates that stretches across the vast ocean of his library.

1   John Dee, marginal note and underlining in *Index eorum, qui hoc in libro habentur, Iamblicus, de mysteriis Aegyptiorum*, ed. and tr. Marsilio Ficino (Venice, Aldus Manutius, 1516), fol. 52v (cat. no. 110).

2   Deborah E. Harkness, *John Dee's Conversations with Angels: Cabala, Alchemy and the End of Nature* (Cambridge, 1999).

3   See esp. Frances A. Yates, *Theatre of the World* (Chicago, IL, 1969); Yates, *The Occult Philosophy in the Elizabethan Age* (London, 1979); and Nicholas Clulee, *John Dee's Natural Philosophy: Between Science and Religion* (New York, 1988).

4   Lily Bess Campbell, *Scenes and Machines on the English Stage During the Renaissance* (Cambridge, 1923), 87.

5   See *John Dee's Library Catalogue*, ed. Julian Roberts and Andrew G. Watson (London, 1990).

6   See the original and important study by William H. Sherman, *John Dee: The Politics of Reading and Writing in the English Renaissance* (Amherst, MA, 1995).

7   See Lisa Jardine and Anthony Grafton, "'Studied for Action': How Gabriel Harvey Read his Livy," *Past & Present*, no. 129 (1990): 30–78.

8   British Library, shelfmark 531.k.6, item 3.

9   Marsilio Ficino, *Three Books on Life*, ed. and tr. Carol V. Kaske and John R. Clark (Binghamton, NY, 1989), 316–17.

10 Fol. 160r.

11 See e.g. Ann Moss, *Printed Commonplace-Books and the Structuring of Renaissance Thought* (Oxford, 1996); Ann Blair, "Annotating and Indexing Natural Philosophy," in *Books and the Sciences in History*, Marina Frasca Spada and Nicholas Jardine, eds. (Cambridge, 2000), 69–89.

12 Celio Calcagnini to Tommaso Calcagnini, n.d., in Calcagnini, *Opera aliquot* (Basel: Froben, 1544), 26.

13 Ibid.

14 The Latin text is in fact much later, and perhaps of North African origin. See *Hermetica*, ed. and tr. Brian P. Copenhaver (Cambridge, 1992), 214.

15 *Asclepius*, chap. 24, tr. ibid., 81.

16 *Asclepius*, chap. 26, tr. ibid., 82–83.

17 See Frances A. Yates, *Giordano Bruno and the Hermetic Tradition* (Chicago, IL, 1964).

18 See Don Cameron Allen, *Mysteriously Meant* (Baltimore, MD, 1970).

19 D. P. Walker, *The Ancient Theology: Studies in Christian Platonism from the Fifteenth to the Eighteenth Century* (London, 1972).

20 For some examples see Lisa Jardine, *Erasmus, Man of Letters: The Construction of Charisma in Print* (Princeton, NJ, 1993).

21 British Library, shelfmark C 54 bb, item 6.

22 Fols. 20r, 20v.

23 Fol. 44v.

24 Ibid.

25 Ibid.; cf. Harkness, chap. 5.

Woodcuts from John Foxe, *Actes and Monuments of . . . great persecutions agaynst the true martyrs . . . Newly revised*, London, by Iohn Daye, 1583. Folger call no. STC 11225.

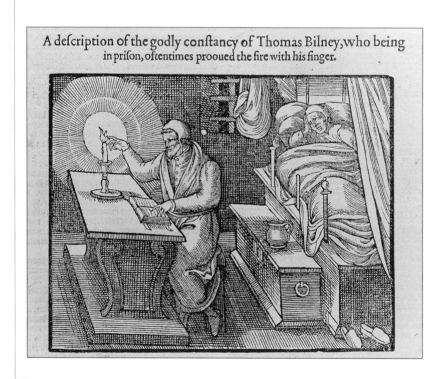

Godly Reading: John Foxe's *Actes and Monuments* (1583)
Evelyn B. Tribble

In April 1571, a Convocation of the English Church meeting at St. Paul's ordered that the "holy Bible in the largest volume as it was lately printed in London and also that full and perfect history which is entitled 'Monuments of Martyrs' be made available in hall or chamber for the use of strangers and servants."[1] The Bible "in the largest volume" is the Bishops' Bible, the revised translation authorized by Elizabeth I in 1568; the 'Monuments of Martyrs' is John Foxe's *Actes and Monuments of These Latter and Perilous Days*, better known as the *Book of Martyrs*. First published in 1563, Foxe's work records the suffering of Protestant martyrs, primarily under the reign of Mary Tudor (1553–57). Subsequent editions, published in 1570, 1576, and 1583, add new records and trace the genealogy of Protestant martyrdom back to apostolic times, in the process swelling the book to well over 2000 folio pages. Although Foxe's work is currently attracting considerable attention from students of early modern English culture, it remains little read and as yet unavailable in a modern edition.[2] It is, however, arguably one of the most important and influential English books ever written. Both in the Elizabethan period and thereafter, the book was reprinted, rewritten, and re-disseminated at moments of perceived crisis in the Protestant church.

Set up in great halls and cathedrals (but not, as is often said, in every parish church in England), Foxe's work provides a gold mine of evidence for reading practices in sixteenth-century England. On one level, it was one of the great public books, available, like the Bible, for reading within certain public spaces and ill-suited by reason of its size and cost for widespread private ownership. Reading in such a setting was likely to be a communal act, and those less skilled at reading might hear the tales read aloud. Indeed, Foxe's work can be seen to appeal to a wide range of literacies. In the 1583 edition, a Latin preface is addressed "ad doctum lectorem." The dedication to Queen Elizabeth asks her "to consider in [the book] the necessity of the ignorant flock of Christ committed to your government in this Realm of England." The numerous woodcuts provided less learned readers with visual witnesses to Papist cruelty and impressed into memory the fortitude of the martyrs. Elaborate typographic tables helped readers organize and synthesize key points, while the marginal glosses liberally used by Foxe guided readers' interpretations of the vast history. In sum, Foxe used all the technological resources of the press to present his history. He believed that the printing press was a gift from God: "By this printing, as by the gift of tongues, and as by the singular organe of the holy Ghost, the doctrine of the Gospell soundeth to all nations and countryes vnder heauen: and what God revealeth to one man, is dispersed to many, and what is knowne in one nation, is opened to all" (707).

The book itself as a physical artifact is testament to the power of the press: it is a literal monument to the ability of the printing press to create social memory. Within the covers of the book, its verbal and visual content continually reinforces the ability of the book and of reading to "disperse" knowledge and "open" the truth to all. For Foxe, the astonishing power of the printing press was manifest through the ability of ordinary men and women to read and understand the scriptures, to internalize their reading through memory, and to deploy their knowledge in a battle of wits with their interrogators. The pages of the *Actes and Monuments* are filled with accounts of the results of such acts of reading.

Reading on the part of ordinary men and women rarely enters the historical records because reading such as this seldom leaves material traces on the page. When such acts of reading are recorded, it is often because of a violation or transgression. Circulating the Bible in English had been outlawed by the Constitutions of Oxford in 1411, and this prohibition was in force until 1538 (and then reinstituted by Mary I upon her accession). In many cases, such violations of laws against the circulation of religious materials and the English Bible provided Foxe with his raw materials: records of arrests, denouncements, and punishments are transformed into documents of heroism and martyrdom. As shall become evident, these readers often did not own the books they read. Instead, reading material was read, imprinted in memory, then circulated to other readers, and often in the end destroyed, either by fearful owners or by the authorities.

In one remarkable set of examples, records attest to the importance of the circulation of books and the existence of a community of readers in Lincolnshire in 1521. Foxe uses a complex table to record the cycle of accusations and denunciations, many of which turned father against son, husband against wife, and brother against brother (Foxe records these moments in the margin). The acts of reading, chronicled in a fourteen-page table, reveal the circulation of books among a small community of readers:

· Thomas Rowland accused John Scriuener the elder "For carrying aboute Bookes from one to another" (823);
· Thomas Holms detected the wife and daughter of Benet Ward "for saying that Thomas Pope was the deuotest manne that euer came in their house, for he woulde sitte readyng in his booke to midnight many times" (824);
· Holms also said that John Butler, Richard Butler, and W. King "sate vp all the night in the house of Durdant of Iuencourte by Stanes, readinge all the nighte of a Booke of Scripture" (824);
· Jenkin Butler appeached his brother John "for reading to hym in a certayne Booke of the Scripture and perswading him to harken to the same" (825);
· Joan Norman accused John Barret "because he was heard in his own house before his wife and mayd there present, to recite the Epistle of S. James: which epistle with many other things, hee had perfectly without book" (826);
· John Phip accused the wife of Robert Pope "for hauing certaine bookes in English, one bound in bourds, and three with parchment couerings, with foure other sheetes of paper

written in English, conteining matter against the Romist Religion" (828);

· John Grosar "confessed that he receaued [a book of the Gospels in English] of Thomas Tykill Masse Prieste in Milkestreete and afterware lente the same booke to Thomas Spenser: which Thomas Spenser with hys wife vsed to read vppon the same. After that it was lent to Job Knight who at length deliuered the boke to the Vicare of Kikemansworth" (829);

· A group of thirteen men and women "were detected, for that they being together in Bruges house in Burford, were reading together in the booke of the exposition of the Apocalyps, and communed concerning the matter of opening the booke with seauen calspes, &c." (832);

· Alice Colins "was a famous woman among them, and had a good memory, & could recite much of ye scriptures and other good bookes; And therefore when any conuenticle of these men did meete at Burford, commonly she was sent for, to recite vnto them the declaration of the x commandements, & the Epistles of Peter, and James" (834).

This cycle of accusation ultimately destroyed the circle of readers. One member burned his books, saying that "he had rather burne his bokes than that his boks should burne him." Those condemned were forced to carry a "fagot of wood" on their shoulders as penance and to carry a piece of wood to a heretic's fire; four "relapsed" and were themselves burnt, including John Scriuener, whose children were required to bear wood to his burning. Throughout this long chronicle, Foxe ensures that his own readers see the significance of the persecution—his marginal notes and tables constantly repeat "for reading the Scriptures in English."

A particularly interesting aspect of this record is that it shows the wide circulation of a relatively small number of banned texts within a community. These books were not simply read; they were pored over, memorized, recited, expounded, and explained, in a network that fluidly combines memory, orality, writing, and reading. Other examples of martyrs under Mary I similarly show the blurring of the lines between oral and literate 'reading' and thus bear out Keith Thomas's argument that we must think of "*literacies*" rather than a monolithic and static "literacy" in this period.[3] Indeed, an interesting feature of Foxe's narrative is that a number of his martyrs were illiterate by virtually any measure, yet were nevertheless able to hear and internalize books through more educated relatives, friends, or neighbors. In the list above, Alice Colins is singled out as a particularly valuable member of the community because of her extraordinary mnemonic powers, making her a walking reference for the faithful. Similar instances from the Marian period further show the fluidity of oral and literate knowledge at the time. We are told of John Maundrell, a husbandman who "was a diligent hearer and a feruent embracer of Gods true Religion, so that he delighted in nothing so muche, as to heare and speak of Gods word, neuer being without the new Testament about him, although he could not read himselfe. But when he came into any company that could reade, his book was always ready, having a very good memory; so that he could recite by hart most places of the new Testame[n]t" (1894). Rawlins White, a fisherman, employed his young son to read to him.

Although he never learned to read himself, he had a "singular gift of memory; so that by the benefite thereof he would & could do that, in vouching and rehearsing of the text, which men of riper and more profound knowledge, by their notes and other helps of memory could very hardly accomplish. In so much that he, vpon the alledging of scripture, very often would cite the booke, the leafe, yea and the very sentence: such was the wonderfull working of God in this simple and vnlearned father" (1117). Memory provided an oral means of constructing aids superior to those employed by the learned, allowing White expertly to negotiate the terrain of the book.⁴ What is interesting in this instance is the text-based nature of White's facility: without being able to decipher in the way we ordinarily understand the textual marks on the page, he nevertheless is presented as having a firm spatial grasp on the Bible, a knowledge of the "leafe, yea and the very sentence."

The acquisition of deep scriptural knowledge by those unable to read, indeed those living on the fringes of society, is perhaps borne out most poignantly by the narrative of Joan Waste, who was blind from birth:

> And when she was about xii or xiii, she learned to knitte hosen and sleeues [and] . . . she would help her father to turn ropes, and do such other things as she was able, and in no case would be idle. . . . [After hearing English sermons during the reign of Edward VI] she became marvellously well affected to the religion then taught. So at length hauing by her labour gotten and saved so much money as would by her a new testame[n]t, she caused one to be prouided for her. And though she was of herselfe unlearned and by reason of her blindness vnable to read, yet for the great desire shee had to vnderstand and haue printed in her memory the sayings of holy scriptures conteined in the new Testament shee acquainted her selfe chiefly with one John Hurt, then prisoner in the common Jail of Darby, for debtes. The Same John Hurt . . . by her earnest intreatie . . . did for his exercise dayly read vnto her some one chapter of the New Testament . . . . Some-times shee would geue a penny or two (as shee might spare) to such persons as would not freely read vnto her, appoyntyng vnto them aforehand how many Chapters of the newe Testament they should read, or how often they should repeate one Chapter vpon a price (1951–52).

As a result of this instruction, achieved through deprivation and hard work, "not only could she recite many chapters of ye Newe Testament without book, but also could aptly impugne, by diuers places of scriptures, as well sinne, as such abuses in Religion, as then were to much in vse, in diuers and sundry persons" (1952). The ability to "impugne" and detect abuses, later displayed in her interrogation by the bishops, is particularly admired in Foxe. The result of learning the Scriptures is not rote memorization, but an ability to negotiate textual places deftly and to deploy that knowledge even—perhaps especially—in the face of great personal danger. Waste was burnt for her refusal to recant.

A final way of thinking about reading in this text is through its visual representation in the woodcuts. At the base of the elaborate woodcut title page that begins each edition of Foxe, Protestant and Catholic modes of learning are contrasted. On the left, a Catholic priest is speaking to a bored audience more preoccupied with its rosary beads than the content of the sermon; the Corpus Christi pageant in the distance reinforces the Catholic obsession with external ceremonies rather than the word of God. On the right, a Protestant preacher speaks while his congregation listens attentively. Prominent in the foreground is a book open on the lap of a woman. The written and the oral word reinforce one another in this visual display of godly reading. Another example that places the book within the context of English history is the woodcut that begins the second volume of the 1583 edition. In a cut that recalls the title page to the Great Bible, Henry VIII is seated on his throne receiving the English Bible from Cromwell and Cranmer, decorously clad in skullcaps (the visual sign of Protestants). Henry's feet rest on the uncrowned Pope Clement VII, who is surrounded by tonsured friars and monks wearing the same foolish expressions as the Papists on the title page. The message is clear: the book and the crown have conquered superstition and error.

The two woodcuts reproduced in the exhibition catalogue provide visual representations of the power of reading and the power of the book for the martyrs Foxe memorializes. In "A Picture describing the maner and place of them which were in *bondes for the testimony of the truth, conferring together among themselues*," we see a visual analogue to the community of readers described in the Lincolnshire indictments. Robert Smith, one hand holding a book open and the other pointing to it, expounds the scripture to a group of imprisoned men and women. Even more powerfully, a cut entitled "A description of the godly constancy of Thomas Bilney, who being in prison, oftentimes prooued the fire with his finger" shows Bilney holding his finger over a flame while reading the scriptural passage: "Whe[n] thou walkest in the fire, it shall not burne thee" (1012). As he contemplates his execution by fire the next day, he tests the power of God's word. Godly reading was more powerful than bodily sensation.

1   Quoted in William Haller, *Foxe's Book of Martyrs and the Elect Nation* (London, 1963). The longstanding legend that the *Book of Martyrs* was available in every parish church is, however, merely legend. See Leslie Oliver, "The Seventh Edition of John Foxe's *Acts and Monuments*," *The Papers of the Bibliographical Society of America* 37 (1943): 243–60.

2   A version of the 1583 edition is now planned. See http://www.shef.ac.uk/uni/projects/bajfp/main/aim.html.

3   Keith Thomas, "The Meaning of Literacy in Early Modern England," in *The Written Word: Literacy in Transition*, Gerd Baumann, ed. (London, 1986).

4   Mary Carruthers has written on the ways that the appearance of the page worked to localize and thus fix memory in the medieval period. See *The Book of Memory: A Study of Memory in Medieval Culture* (Cambridge, 1990).

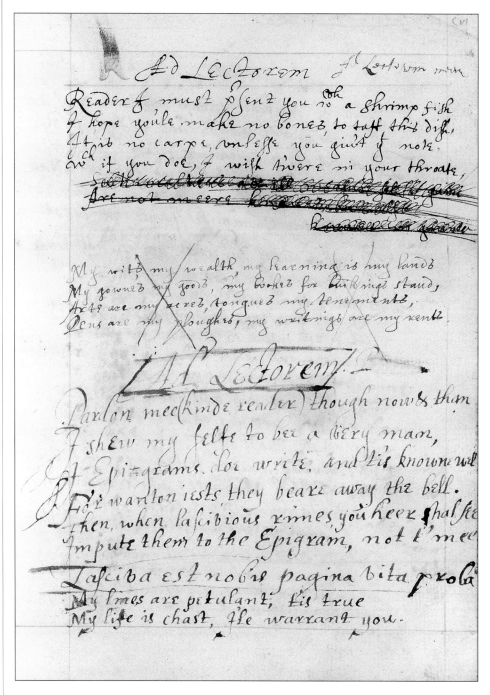

Ad Lectorem

Reader I must present you wth a shrimp fish
I hope youle make no bones, to tast this dish,
It is no carpe, vnlesse you giu't yt note,
wch if you doe, I wish t'were in your throate,

~~scratched out lines~~
~~Are not in eere~~

My wit's my wealth, my learning is my lands
My gownes my goods, my bookes for building stand,
Arts are my acres, tongues my tenements,
Pens are my ploughes, my writings are my rents.

Ad Lectorem

Pardon mee (kinde reader) though now & then
I shew my selfe to bee a very man,
If Epigrams I doe write, and 'tis knowne well
For wanton iests, they beare away the bell.
Then, when lascibious rimes, you heere shal see
Impute them to the Epigram, not t'mee

Lasciva est nobis pagina vita proba
My lines are petulant, 'tis true
My life is chast, I'le warrant you.

A page from Commonplace Book, Manuscript, ca. 1630 (cat. no. 101).

Folger MSS V.a. 89 and V.a. 345: Reading Lyric Poetry in Manuscript

Arthur F. Marotti

In England during the first two and one-half centuries of print culture, the older system of textual transmission in manuscript remained vigorous. It allowed material to circulate that would have been changed or suppressed by the mechanisms of official censorship governing the print industry. It suited authors who, perhaps, wished to avoid the social degradation associated with the democratizing forces operating within print publication.[1] It was also congenial to writers and readers who wished to limit texts to circuits of transmission within the family or other restricted social circles.[2] Manuscript transmission of texts took the form of letters, bifolia, small quires, or larger gatherings of material.[3] Material was compiled in personal albums or 'commonplace books' by individuals or by groups of collectors. Many of these compilations consist of a wide range of miscellaneous material copied from both printed and manuscript sources, including literary texts, medical receipts, personal journal or diary entries, household accounts, and excerpts from historical, theological, moral, and philosophical readings.[4]

Many texts that have come down to us as 'literary' ones, especially lyric poems, were either originally designed by their authors for manuscript circulation (the poems of Sir Philip Sidney and John Donne, for example) or continued to be transmitted and collected in manuscript even after their print publication. The composition, transmission, and collection of lyrics was associated with such social environments as the royal court, the universities, the Inns of Court, and aristocratic and middle-class households. The two manuscripts of poetry considered in this essay represent some of this variety: the first, Folger MS V.a. 89, is a collection of mid-Elizabethan courtly poetry owned by an aristocratic woman related to Edward de Vere, seventeenth earl of Oxford; the second, Folger MS V.a. 345, is a very large compilation of Jacobean and Caroline poetry and some prose, belonging to a man who had connections to Christ Church, Oxford, an environment that generated a large number of poetical anthologies in the 1620s and 1630s.[5] The differences in gender of the owners are reflected in the contents of the two documents.

Folger MS V.a. 89 is a booklet originally owned by Anne Cornwallis, daughter of Sir William Cornwallis and his wife Lucy, the daughter of Lord Latimer. She was a distant relative of the earl of Oxford by way of a family line going back to John Vere.[6] The document comprises two sets of material: the first six pages contain unique copies of seven poems composed by John Bentley, written in a non-professional secretary hand, possibly that of the author; the next twenty-seven pages contain a small collection of Elizabethan courtly verse—mostly from the 1570s through the mid-1580s—transcribed in a single, neat, professional secretary hand. As William H. Bond has observed, "It is very much as if the book had been used for two different purposes at different times and by different people."[7] Both sections of the manuscript contain the kind of amorous verse current in Elizabethan courtly and polite society.

The Bentley poems, written both in pentameter and in the old-fashioned meters of early Elizabethan poetry (poulter's measure and "fourteeners")[8] are plaintive love poems, some alluding to a courtly context. The second Bentley poem, for example, is spoken in the voice of a man exiled from court:

> If I might change my forme . and god anewe mee make .
> the shape of simple flie I wold . no other body take .
> not for he lives in place . whear mighty princes bee
> and putt his feete in bed & dish with men of best degree
> but for because hee can . kisse when his list a queene
> and lay the fayrest dame on lipps . that earst was ever seene
> yet when the winter comes . his danger drawes apace
> well may hee die by good consent . that found such happy grace .
> but I alas ame lyke . the Aunte or blinded moulde
> that in the winter keeps their cave . whear they no sun behold
> whose lives but lingered owt, in darknes half the year .
> and I such duringe sorrowes tast . as tyme can never wear .
>
> (p. 1)[9]

In such a piece, political fortunes are encoded in the vocabulary of love, a familiar Elizabethan strategy.[10] Most of the other Bentley poems speak in a Petrarchan vocabulary more directly about love and the ill fortunes of the (male) lover: "nothinge but death the hatefull coles can quench/ that breede by love . and kindle myne unrest" (Poem #3, ll. 11–12; p.2); "my hope & helpe . doth rest in hir alone/ whose love first causde my greefe . my plainte & endles mone" (Poem #6, ll. 5–6; p. 5); "yf I shuld weepe & weale my woes till death ./ my mistress wold not once behould my payne,/ no meanes I finde . by god & by my faythe/ to win her love" (Poem #7, ll. 1–4; p. 5).[11] Although these pieces all speak a courtly language accessible to both men and women, one can see how an aristocratic woman might be interested in having them in her book.

From a socio-cultural vantage point, it is the miscellaneous collection of courtly verse in the second part of the manuscript that is more important, for it not only contains twenty-seven interesting courtly poems, nine of which exist here in apparently unique texts,[12] but it highlights women's participation in the manuscript transmission and collection of lyric verse, their interest in the poetry of polite courtly amorousness and, in this particular case, a fascination with poems related to a notorious court sex scandal, the affair between the earl of Oxford and Anne Vavasor (a Gentlewoman of the Bedchamber to Queen Elizabeth I). The affair produced an illegitimate child in 1581.[13] The courtly poems in this second part of the manuscript include pieces by Sir Philip Sidney, Sir Edward Dyer, Sir Walter Ralegh, Francis Edwards, Oxford, and Sir William Cordell. One lyric, "When that thine eye hath chose the dame" (pp. 25–26) has been attributed to William Shakespeare—though this is disputable.[14] The Sidney and Dyer poems represent work from a famous literary coterie that also included Fulke Greville and Edmund Spenser. Two poems were part of a literary competition or a poem-and-answer set, Sidney's "A satyre once did runne away for dread" (p. 23; subscribed "S p. sydney") and Dyer's "Prometheus when first from heaven hye" (p. 21; subscribed "Dier").

The two poems subscribed "Vavaser" seem to be associated with the disgraced maid of honor's affair with the earl of Oxford. One of these, "Sittinge alone upon my thought in melancholye moode" (p. 13), may have been written by Oxford himself, even though the second part of the poem represents the voice of the distraught beloved (who says things flattering to his ego). The other poem, "Thoughe I seeme strange sweete frynd be thou not soe" (pp. 8–9) may, in fact, be by Anne herself, though British Library MS Harley 6910 identifies it as "La[dy] B. to N."[15] This piece clearly expresses love from the point of view of a courtly woman fearful of scandal, gossip, and the loss of her good name. It utilizes some very old codes of courtly love—especially in evoking the danger of envious gossipers who would harm the reputation of the woman forced to display shamefastness and a cheerful social behavior ("to cloke my sad conceiptes with smyling cheare") even as she concealed her love and suffered its pangs. The speaker thus apologizes to her lover for her standoffish behavior, assuring him of her fidelity: "my hearte hathe vowed althoughe my tonge sayes no. . . . he [hath] my harte whom most I seme to hate." This lyrical expression of feeling is a prelude to a deliberate avoidance of all communication with her lover—"thou shalte not heare by worde or writinge oughte," assuring him, however, of her unchangeable "vowe." The fragility of a female reputation and honor in a courtly setting was a constant theme in the literature of the time: in Anne Vavasor's case, one of Elizabeth's female attendants became the object of the queen's and the court's social disapproval as both Oxford's and Anne's reputations and courtly careers suffered serious damage from their affair once their child was born. Anne Cornwallis, then, could read such stylish courtly verse not simply as elegant literary amorousness, but also as all-too-relevant communication in the social environment in which she participated. Her connection to Oxford's lineage would seem partly to explain her interest in having copies of these poems and of the other poem in the collection ventriloquizing a female voice, the famous lyric portraying Queen Elizabeth as an aging woman repenting her rejection of amorous suitors, "When I was faire and yonge" (p. 12), subscribed here "l. of oxforde."[16]

The last piece in the manuscript is a much-transcribed political poem referring to the French Civil wars, "The state of France" (pp. 32–33), which appealed to the anti-Catholic English because of the villainous reputation of the militant-Catholic Guise faction. Based on a French lyric and composed about the year 1585, this piece, as Steven May has shown, was copied over an extended period of time into a range of manuscript collections, some of them chronologically quite distant from the immediate topical circumstance of the French power struggles that preceded the accession of Henry of Navarre as Henry IV.[17]

In early modern England, one of the most favorable environments for the production of poetry was the university. Students rhetorically trained from an early age in poetic composition in both Latin and the vernacular during their university years both wrote and collected verse, compiling either personal or group anthologies of poems of interest to them or their fellows. Although students at both Oxford and Cambridge engaged in verse-collection and composition, some colleges were noteworthy for fostering these practices. Of these, Christ Church, Oxford, in the 1620s and 1630s, perhaps, is the best example. This was due primarily to two factors: (1) the high percentage of students coming from Westminster School, whose Master, William Osbaldson, encouraged poetic composition;[18] and (2) the poetic activities of Richard Corbet, William Strode, George Morley, and other poets connected to Christ Church.[19]

Folger MS V.a. 345 is a 337-page manuscript written in the single hand of a person with Christ Church, Oxford, connections in the 1620s, or a professional scribe employed by him.[20] The last poem in the collection concerns the death of George Villiers, first duke of Buckingham, in 1628.[21] One of the largest anthologies of poetry (over five hundred poems) to be found in the manuscripts traceable to the socio-literary milieu of Christ Church in the late Jacobean and Caroline periods, it contains much verse that was later printed in the poetical miscellanies appearing between 1640 and 1660.[22] But it also has a number of prose items, including forty-five characters by John Earle (pp. 184–218) that were circulating in manuscript before their initial publication;[23] a long section of medical receipts (pp. 246–68); a satiric travel letter from Scotland (pp. 37–42); a letter to Queen Elizabeth I (p. 96); and an anecdote about a minister and three drunks (p. 180).

The collection contains a number of poems from outside the Oxford environment, some of them written much earlier. Lyrics by, possibly by, or misattributed to John Donne include "When I di'd last" ("The Legacie," p. 74); "Dr. Dunne to his Mrs going to bed," (Elegy 19, pp. 80–81); "Loves Dyet" (pp. 146–47); stanza two of "Loves Diety" (p. 146); "Since she must goe" (Elegy 21, pp. 88–89); "Dr Dunne on his Departure from his Love" ("Dearest Love, I doe not goe," pp. 131–32); "Dr Dunne of his Mrs rising" ("Ly stil my deare why doest thou rise," p. 237, which includes one stanza of "Break of Day"); Sir Henry Wotton's poem "Happy is he borne & taughte" (p. 63); "Dr Dunne, one the death of his Mrs," ("Is death so great a gamster, that he throwes," pp. 82–84, by William Browne); and a poem written in imitation of Donne's "A Valediction: Forbidding Mourning" ("The man and wife that kinde and loving are," pp. 44–45). Though not represented by a large collection of his verse, such as one might find in other manuscript anthologies of the period, Donne is a significant presence in this collection, signaling the strong interest that the Oxford community had in the person and writings of the witty poet who had become dean of St. Paul's. At the bottom of page 106 of the manuscript is a version of the whimsical statement composed after Donne's marriage to Anne More cost him his position in the government: "John Donne, Anne Donne, undonne at London."

Other poets from outside the university community whose earlier or contemporary work is included in the collection include Sir Walter Ralegh, represented by four lyrics ("What is our life," p. 14; "Even such is time," p. 32; "In obitum Ro[bert] Cecilii" ["Here lyes old Hobbinol"], p. 110; and "Goe soule the bodies guest," pp. 176–77); Ben Jonson (three pieces: "Ben John[son] The Divells feast" ["Cooke Lorell would needs have the devell his guest"], pp. 178–79; "Drink to me only with thine eyes," p. 286; and "A Lover" ["Kysse me sweete the wary love"], pp. 286–87); Sir John Davies ("On Cate," p. 305); Joshua Sylvester ("To a Gentlewoman" ["Beware faire maide of musky Courtiers oathes"], pp. 292–93); Robert Southwell, S. J. ("Of the Blessed Saviour's Flyght to Egypt," p. 70); William Drummond of Hawthornden ("Of the five senses by James Johnson," p. 59); Sir Robert Ayton ("Wrong not sweet Empress of my hart," pp. 90–91); Sir Francis Bacon ("The worlds a buble," pp. 143–44); Sir Henry Wotton ("On the Queen of Bohemia," pp. 148–49, and the poem attributed to Donne); and Chidiock Tichborne ("Mr Tichbornes Elegy in the tower," p. 284). This manuscript is one of a very few containing examples of Shakespeare's poetry, here the version of Sonnet 2 entitled "Spes Altera A Song" (p. 144) and the satiric epitaph on a usurer, "Shakespeare on S[i]r Joh[n] Coome" (p. 232).[24] In addition to these, there are some half-dozen poems by Thomas Carew, whose verse circulated in manuscript before its posthumous publication in 1640 ("Goe thou gentle whispering wind," p. 10; "An excuse for absence," p. 28; "Dearest thy tresses," p. 92; "A Gentle[man] to his mistres," pp. 151–52; "Palinodia Loves Folly," pp. 152–53; "A Song" ["In your fair cheeks 2 pitts doe ly"], pp. 293–94).

The collector had a real fondness for satiric epigrams. He included a large number of pieces by Thomas Bastard (pp. 4–5, 49–51); Sir John Harington (pp. 13, 30–31, 51–52, and 103); Henry Fitzjeffrey (pp. 52–55, 79, 82); John Owen (pp. 238–40); and Thomas Freeman (pp. 171–75). All of these may have been drawn from printed editions.[25] They are combined in the collection with the many other comic epitaphs and short satiric items, some of which are directly related to the university milieu—for example, pieces on John Dawson, the butler of Christ Church (p. 147); "On the Dene of Allsoules slaine with a Jugge by Benford" (p. 150); "Not upon Egerly the Carriers wife but uppon Egerlyes wife the carrier" (pp. 225–26); "On Brasenose Coll[ege]" (p. 280); "On the President of St. Johns" (p. 124); "On him that took a way some of the university lands and afterward new Plaster'd the Schooles" (p. 134, on George Ryves, Warden of New College, who died in 1613); and "An Elme given by the President of St. Johns" (p. 274).

As might be expected, the poetry collection contains many poems by Christ Church and other Oxford poets. Richard Corbet, dean of Christ Church, is represented by some eighteen items, including poems to his patron Buckingham ("A Newyeares gift to the Duke of Bucking-hamshire," p. 124) and a piece on Buckingham's and Prince Charles's journey into Spain in 1623 to negotiate a marriage with the Infanta ("Dr Corbet of the Princes jorney into Spain," pp. 135–36).[26] Another much-collected Christ Church poet, William Strode, is represented by five lyrics.[27] Other poets include Daniel Price, Brian Duppa, Benjamin Stone, Jeramiel Terrent, Edward Lapworth, and Henry King (whose much transcribed elegy for his wife, "The Exequie," appears in this manuscript, pp. 104–6).

A large number of poems in the anthology refer to events and personages connected with the university and its surrounding community. For example, several scandals and public embarrassments are memorialized: the 30 January 1626 conviction for embezzle-ment and subsequent royal pardon of John Clavell, purser of Brasenose College (p. 25); the disastrous presentation of the Christ Church author Barten Holiday's play *Technogamia* before King James I at Woodstock, 26 August 1620 (pp. 140–42); the Proctor's Plot of 1626 (p. 23); and the event that caused the dean of Christ Church to become a standing joke in the university, the sermon Corbet preached before King James during which, because he was fiddling with a ring the king had just given him, he forgot the text of his sermon and could not continue (pp. 133–34). Other poems celebrate or memorialize members of the Oxford community. There are poems "On Dr Corbets Marriage" (pp. 297–300); on the death of the earl of Pembroke's chaplain, Mr. John Smith of Magdalen College (p. 283); and on "the untimely [1625] death of Mr John Stanhop sonne and heire to the honourable Lord Stanhop" (p. 150), the last composed by Edward Radcliffe of University College, who also wrote a poem on the death of the physician Samuel Johnson (p. 18). Another poem mourns the 1619 death of Dr. Bartholomew Warner (p. 124). There are three poems about the 1626 death of Mr. James Vaux, professor of medicine, suggesting (along with the extensive list of medical receipts included in this manuscript) that the compiler of Folger V.a. 345 might have been a physician.[28] One poem mocks Christ Church poets for their inept elegies on the topic of Sir Henry Savile's death.[29] Finally, two poems take notice of the "town" surrounding the world of the "gown": "Mr Samborne Sheriff of Oxford" (p. 14), by Benjamin Stone and "On Sir Francis Stonor Recusant Shreif of Oxford the assize being on Shrove-tuesday 1622" (pp. 138–39), the second satirically connecting the Catholic sheriff's stinginess and his religion.

With regard to religion, the collection has a significant number of anti-Catholic pieces. These include "The Pope's Pater Noster" (p. 37); "A Papist Creed" (p. 37); a poem about the

Blackfriars' disaster of 1623, in which a room collapsed killing many among the hundreds of people who had come to hear a Jesuit preach ("Goe to ye sons of Antichrist," p. 42); "In fisherie" (p. 43); "The Blazon" (p. 97); "On Church who beat a fencer at all weapons" (p. 149); and "An Answere to the song against blackcoats" (referring to an anti-Catholic ballad about clerical lechery, p. 157). But the popular anti-Puritan lyrics "The conference of 6 puritanical wenches" ("Six of the weaker sex but purer sect," p. 43) and "A zealous sister with one of her society" (p. 47) also found their way into the anthology.

Numerous topical and political poems are scattered throughout the collection. Some deal with the deaths or falls of royals, aristocrats, or lesser social and political figures. Poems mourn the loss of Queen Elizabeth (pp. 110, 111); King James (p. 80, 155–56, 273); his wife, Queen Anne (pp. 71, 72–73); the duke of Lennox (pp. 305–6); Lady Elizabeth Ruddier (pp. 274–75); Lady Frances Mildmay (pp. 309–10); and Sir Robert Berkeley (p. 236). Other pieces are satiric memorials: the poems on Robert Cecil, first earl of Salisbury's 1612 death ("Fayre Ladyes howle yee and cry," p. 36); on Lady Rich (p. 9); on Lady Lake (p. 285); and on the duke of Buckingham (p. 315). There are three pieces about the impeached Lord Chancellor, Francis Bacon, viscount St. Alban's (pp. 127–31) and one about another impeachment victim, Sir Giles Mompeson (p. 126). Another poem concerns the jailing of the outspoken MPs from the Addled Parliament of 1614 (p. 96). Two poems deal with the ill political fortunes of Arbella Stuart: "Andr[ew] Melvin, to Mr Seamore committed to the Tower for the marriage of the Lady Arbella" (p. 103), and Corbet's "On the lady Arabella" ("How doe I thank the death, and blesse that power," p. 143). One satirically nasty poem deals with the scandal surrounding the marriage of Robert Carr, first earl of Somerset, to the divorced Frances Howard, "On the Lady Carr" ("There was at court a ladye of late," p. 290), a piece that is found in many other manuscript collections.

Although contemporary university affairs and political events captured the attention of the compiler of Folger MS V.a. 345, by far the largest number of poems deal with love and sex, his tastes often running to the bawdy. The anthology contains many snobbish or misogynistic poems about women and amorous experience. To some extent, the collection culturally embodies a gynophobic, patriarchal point of view. Many of its comic and satiric pieces are directed against women and assert a strong masculine bias—for example, "An Invective against women" (p. 35); "A Shrew" (p. 46); "In disprayse of women" (p. 58); "A Song in disprayse of women" (pp. 67–68); "Of a woman" ("Commit thy selfe unto the winde," p. 168); "If yee that Lovers bee, and love the amorous trade" (p. 291); and a bawdy piece later crossed out:

> An Epitapht on <a whore>
> <Here lyes her inclosed in brick
> That living burned many a prick,
> I pray thee therefore, for her greater honor
> Pull out thy prick and pisse uppon her>
>
> (p. 9)[30]

Poems of comic wooing include the anti-Welsh piece, "The Loving Welshman" (pp. 31–32); "A Country suter to his love" (p. 34); and the song about the rustic man's suit to a sophisticated city woman ("Sweethart I love thee," pp. 77–78). Outright bawdy pieces include the much transcribed dialogue poem, "Nay pish, nay pu, In fayth but will you? Fie" (pp. 7–8); "A medication for the greene sickness" (p. 47); a poem about a sexual encounter following a man's finding a naked woman bathing ("Uppon a summers day, bout the middle of the morne," p. 171); a poem about another sexually compliant woman ("On Philomel," p. 273); one about a whore ("Say litle one, Canst thou love mee," p. 289); and "My mistres loves no woodcock" (p. 290).

Many songs, usually dealing with the subject of love, have been transcribed in this manuscript, sometimes from printed sources.[31] There is a long poem, beginning "Leander on the banks," which the scribe began copying on pages 63–65, then referred to its completion on page 240. A run of songs and ballads is found on pages 161–67.[32] The presence of these pieces reminds us that we are dealing with an age in which the separation of lyric poetry from music was not as sharp as it was in later periods.

Folger MS V.a. 345, then, reflects tastes and collecting habits of an Oxford-educated, politically aware man of the late Jacobean and early Caroline period. The five hundred or so poems and miscellaneous prose copied into his collection include both frivolous and serious pieces, topical and ephemeral as well as more culturally durable works, aesthetically fine poetry as well as silly doggerel, bigoted and misogynistic pieces along with intellectually engaging items. The compiler prefaces the manuscript with three poems addressed to whoever reads his collection, defending its less edifying contents for their recreative value in a life of serious business. After a poem announcing his taste for epigrams (p. v) and quoting and translating Martial's defense of the form—"Lasciva [sic] est nobis pagina vita proba" ("My lines are petulant, t'is true/ My life is chast, I'le warrant you" [p. v])—he presents the justification for his anthology in the longest of these poems:

Ad Lectoram

Some may perchance account my time mispent

And mee unwise to write such things as these

But let them know my deed Ile ne're repent

Twas not for profit but my selfe to please

For though most profit gaines most commendation

Yet sometime must be spent in recreation

He that most busied is, somtime will finde

As interims freed from serious affayres

Wherein to recreate his dulled minde

Not able to endure continual cares

The vilest miser he that never spares

To search and scrape for gold, hath in his fashion

Seasons selected for his recreation

Then let not any this as idle deeme

Whose only end was idlenes to shun

Lest being more busy they most idle seeme

Condemning, never thinking why twas done

But if such Momists hither needs wil come

This is my answer to such peevish elves

I laugh to see them selves displease themselves

(p. vi)

He claims that his pleasurable private recreation has redeeming psychological and social value and, as these poems to the reader indicate, he believes others will find the collection beneficial.

Like Folger MS V.a. 89, MS V.a. 345 contains a large number of poems whose authors we cannot identify.[33] The anthology is both personal and socially connected to the reading and collecting habits of university and professional men of the early-seventeenth century, demonstrating the ways texts of poetry and literary prose were embedded in the social environments where they functioned. 'Literature,' in such a system of manuscript composition, transmission, and collection, was not separated from ordinary experience and a larger field of discourse the way it came to be in the following three centuries. Both Folger manuscripts are the relics of a time when literary texts had a different ontological and social status from the one they came to have in a highly-developed print culture.

1   See J. W. Saunders, "The Stigma of Print: A Note on the Social Bases of Tudor Poetry," *Essays in Criticism* 1 (1951): 139–64.

2   See the discussion of the system of manuscript transmission and collection of lyric poetry in my book, *Manuscript, Print, and the English Renaissance Lyric* (Ithaca and London, 1995).

3   For a discussion of practices of manuscript transmission and circulation, see Harold Love, *Scribal Publication in Seventeenth-Century England* (Oxford, 1993).

4   For an account of the uses of commonplace books as ways of recording and preserving knowledge and one's individual intellectual equipment for living, see Mary Thomas Crane, *Framing Authority: Sayings, Self, and Society in Sixteenth-Century England* (Princeton, NJ, 1993).

5   These include British Library MSS Additional 30982, 58215, Egerton 2421, and Sloane 1792; Bodleian Library MSS English Poetry e.14 and e.30; Rosenbach Library (Philadelphia) MS 239/22 and 239/27; Westminster Abbey MS 41; and Folger MSS V.a. 97, V.a. 170, V.a. 262, and V.b. 43. For a discussion of Christ Church anthologies and their relationships, see Mary Hobbs, *Early Seventeenth-Century Verse Miscellany Manuscripts* (Aldershot, 1992), 82–85 and 116–23.

6   An (nineteenth-century?) owner of V.a. 89 has inserted a family tree for Anne Cornwallis to demonstrate her connection to that lineage.

7   "The Cornwallis-Lysons Manuscript and the Poems of John Bentley," in *Joseph Quincy Adams Memorial Studies*, James G. McManaway, Giles E. Dawson, and Edwin E. Willoughby, eds. (Washington, DC, 1948), 686.

8   The third, fifth, and seventh poems are pentameter (#5 a sonnet); the first, second, and sixth poems are in poulter's measure (couplets each constructed of a seven-stress line followed by a six-stress line), and the fourth poem is in fourteeners (couplets with lines of seven stresses each).

9   I use Bond's transcription of this lyric, including his reproduction of the caesural periods used by the scribe.

10   For a discussion of the connections of amorous language and political ambition, see my essay, "'Love is not love': Elizabethan Sonnet Sequences and the Social Order," *English Literary History* 49 (1982): 396–428.

11   I quote from the transcriptions of Bond, 688–91.

12   In order, these are (listed by their first lines): "Come sweet delighte & comforte carefull mynde" (p. 16); "A theife was hanged of late yow hearde" (p. 18); "By due desertes deme all my deedes which sheweth every fruite" (p. 20); "Content above from god is sente" (p. 21); "Ye heavenly gods pertakers be with me" (p. 24); "What meanest thou hope to breed me such myshappe" (p. 27); "Harde is his happe who leades his lyfe by losse" (p. 28); "Passe gentell thoughtes to her whom I love beste" (pp. 28–29); "I often wyshe it were not done" (p. 30). Steven W. May has kindly checked their first lines in the data base of his forthcoming *Bibliography and First-Line Index of English Verse, 1559–1603*, confirming that these poems are unique copies.

13   Bond, 685–86, notes "the notorious affair between Oxford and Vavasour . . . became a public scandal in 1581, the echoes reverberating some four or five years longer." Cf. the discussion of Anne Vavasor in E. K. Chambers, *Sir Henry Lee: An Elizabethan Portrait* (Oxford, 1936), 150–62. Oxford ruined his chances for preferment by this indiscretion; later Sir Walter Ralegh deeply offended the queen by his clandestine marriage to one of her maids of honor, Elizabeth Throckmorton, an act that caused a precipitous decline in his fortunes.

14 Of the nine poems to which names or initials are subscribed, three are attributed to Dyer, two to Oxford, two to Anne Vavasor, and one each to Sidney and "G. M." These ascribed poems include: "Weare I a kinge" ("Vere finis") (p. 7); "Thoughe I seeme strange" ("finis Vavaser") (pp. 8–9); "I woulde it were not as it is" ("dyer") (pp. 9–10); "When I was faire and yonge" ("l. of oxforde") (p. 12); "Sittinge alone" ("Vavaser") (p.13); "My care to keepe" ("G. M.") (pp. 14–15); "Prometheus when" ("dier") (p. 21); "Wher one would be" ("finis Dier") (p. 23); "A satyre once" ("finis S p. sydney") (p. 23). Some unascribed poems can be identified: "The saylinge shippe with Ioy, at length doth touche their longe desired porte" (Francis Edwards) (p. 7); "farewell false love thow oracle of lyes" (Ralegh) (pp. 10–11); "As rare to heare as seldom to be seene" (Dyer) (p. 17); "Calling to mynde myne eye went long aboute" (Ralegh) (p. 19); and "Wher one woulde be ther not to be" (Dyer) (p. 22). One other can only problematically be assigned: "when that thyne eye hath chose the dame" (possibly Shakespeare) (pp. 25–26). For these identifications, see Bond, 691–93. The poem subscribed "G. M." is by Sir William Cordell. It also appears in the Arundel-Harington Manuscript (see *The Arundel Harington Manuscript of Tudor Poetry*, ed. Ruth Hughey, 2 vols. [Columbus, OH, 1960], 1: 353–54). I am grateful to Steven W. May for this reference.

15 Margaret Crum, *First-Line Index of Manuscript Poetry in the Bodleian Library*, 2 vols. (New York, 1969), 2: 937, notes also *RP* 85, fol. 17; *RP* 172, fol. 5v. It also appears in Harl. 7392, fol. 40.

16 In *Elizabeth I, Collected Works*, ed. Leah S. Marcus, Janel Mueller, and Mary Beth Rose. (Chicago and London, 2000), 303, the editors, noting that the poem is attributed to the queen in Harl. 7392, fol. 21v and Bodleian MS Rawlinson Poetical 85, fol. 1, want to accept this piece as hers in order to make it evidence of her "poetic range," but its message would seem to be more a fantasy of a male courtier than the queen's genuine regret for withholding her love. It may, in fact, be by Oxford.

17 For a discussion of this poem see Steven W. May, "'The French Primero': A Study in Renaissance Textual Transmission and Taste," *English Language Notes* 9 (1971): 102–8; L. G. Black and Curt Bühler, "Four Elizabethan Poems," in *Joseph Quincy Adams Memorial Studies*, 704.

18 For a discussion of Westminster-Christ Church connections, see Raymond Anselment, "The Oxford University Poets and Caroline Panegyric," *John Donne Journal* 3 (1984): 184–86.

19 Other Oxford poets whose work was collected in Christ Church anthologies include Henry King, Daniel Price, Benjamin Stone, and Jeramial Terrent.

20 The whole book is ruled to provide top, bottom, and side margins. At the end of the manuscript there are four blank pages with ruling, but no text. The original numbering begins after six preliminary pages and continues to p. 244, at the bottom of which are two lines of ornamental marks. Page 245 is blank and what follows is an originally unpaginated 23-page section of medical receipts, followed by a prose "character," before the poetry anthology resumes with the scribally marked page 245. I follow the Folger pencil numbering of pages, starting with the beginning of the prose section and running to the end of the manuscript.

21 A better fix on the date or dates of transcription might be by way of checking the contents against the texts of the poems it shares with *Wits Recreations* (1640) and Carew's 1640 poems. There is also a song, p. 25, drawn from Richard Zouch's play *The Sophister*, which, Alfred Harbage, *Annals of English Drama 975–1700*, rev. S. Schoenbaum (London, 1964), 128, lists as performed at Oxford sometime between 1610 and 1631 (later published by Humphrey Moseley in 1639). There is also a song from Richard Brome's play, *The Northern Lasse*, which seems to have been licensed for performance in July 1629 (Harbage, 124). I find no certain event referred to in the manuscript nor work in it that can be dated later than 1630. Most of the public events referred to in the manuscript belong to the 1610s and 1620s: for example, the deaths of Prince Henry (1612), Robert Cecil, earl of Salisbury (1612), Sir Walter Ralegh (1618), Queen Anne (1619), the duke of Lennox (1624), King James (1625), and the duke of Buckingham (1628).

22 This collection has many items that appeared later, for example, in the 1637 edition of William Camden's *Remaines* and in *Wits Recreations* (1640). Its contents overlap to a great degree with such manuscripts as Bodleian MSS English Poetry e. 14, Douce f.5, Donation d.58, Corpus Christi College 328, and Malone 19. A check against other Christ Church manuscripts in other archives would, I am sure, reveal many other affinities.

23 John Earle, *Micro-cosmographie, Or, a peece of the world discovered; in essays and characters* (1628).

24 For a discussion of the appearance of the sonnet in manuscript, see Gary Taylor, "Some Manuscripts of Shakespeare's Sonnets," *Bulletin of the John Rylands Library* 68 (1985–86): 210–46.

25 See Thomas Bastard, *Christeloros. Seven bookes of Epigrames* (1598); John Harington, *The most elegant and wittie epigrams of Sir J. Harrington* (1618); Henry Fitzjeffrey, *Satyres and Satyrcall Epigrams* (1617); John Owen, *Epigrammatum libri tres* (1607); and Thomas Freeman, *Rubbe, and a great cast: Epigrams* (1614). The Owen epigrams are translated from Latin into English in the manuscript.

26 The other Corbet poems are: "On Mr. Bolden" ("If gentlenes could tame the fates, or wit," p. 5); the last section of his poem "On the Lady Haddington" (p. 6); "Verses written on a Lute she that owed it being absent" ("Pretty lute when I am gon," p. 9); "Do[ctor] Corbet on Tom the great bel of C.C." ("Be dumbe you infant chimes thumpe not the mettal," pp. 20–22); "On the death of Lady Hay" ("Deare losse, to tel the world I greive, were true," pp. 84–85); "Dr Corbet on Dr Ravis" ("When I past Paules & traveled in the walke," p. 93); "An Invocation of the Ghost of Robert Wisdom" ("Thou once a body now but Ayre," p. 96); "In obitum Domini Thomae Overbury" ("Hadst thou (like others knights of worth"), p. 106); "Antidotum Caecilianum" ("When that rich soul of thine (now sainted) kept," p. 107—not included in Trevor-Roper's edition of Corbett); "Mr. Corbet ag[ainst] Dr Price Aniversaryes On Prince Henry" ("Even so dead Hector," p. 111); "A Reply to the Defence" ("Nor is it griev'd (grave youth) the memory," p. 112); "Dr Corbet to Mr Aylesbury on the Comet ibis" ("My brother and much more had'st thou been mine," pp. 113–14); "In Eandam Dr Corbet" ("Have I renounc't my fayth, or basely sold," p. 123); "Dr Corbet on Com:" ("A Star of late appear'd in Virgoes traine," p. 139); "On the lady Arabella" ("How doe I thank the death, and blesse that power," p. 143); and "On John Dawson Butler at C. C." ("Dawson the Butlers dead although I think," p. 147).

27 "A Watch borrowed of Mrs Elizabeth King" ("Go and count her better houres," p. 63); "On Dr Hut[ton's] daughter of C. C. by W. Stro[de]" ("I saw faire Cloris walk alone," p. 144); "A Song of the Caps" ("The wit hath long beholding been," pp. 228–31); "On a Gentlewoman that sung very wel" ("Be silent you still musick of the spheares," p. 278); "On a Butcher that married a tanners daughter" ("A fitter match could ne're ha'been," p. 297).

28 "On Mr Vaux, who dyed the last lent 1626" (pp. 291–92); "Memoriae Sacrum To the memory of the most worthy and happy professor of Physick, Mr James Vaux of Marston A Comparison between him and Aesculapius" (p. 303–4); and "In Obitum Jacobi Vaulx medici" (p. 314).

29 "S[I]r Raignolds./Christ church poetical-fantastick Braines made tragical verses on the death of S[I]r Henry Savil. These censure them for it" ("Great Tacitus I must lament thy fall"), pp. 87–88.

30 There are several poems or parts of poems crossed out or censored after their initial transcription. See, for example, the pieces wholly or partly deleted on pp. 27 ("A rustick swaine was cleaving of a block"); 34 ("Fayre wench I can not court thye sprightly eyes"); 47 ("Ridle me ridle me what is this/Jack holds in hand when he doth pisse"); 49 ("Are women fayre yea wondrous fayre to see too"); 98 ("This valiant champion whom ambition strove").

31 For example, Thomas Lodge's "Now I see lookes are fained" (pp. 137–38), which appeared in *Musick of Sundrie Kindes* (1607); "Love if a god thou art then evermore thou must," which is found in both *A Poetical Rapsody* (1602) and Robert Jones's *First Set of Madrigals* (1607). I am indebted to Margaret Crum's *First-Line Index* for these references.

32 Other songs appear on pp. 147, 224–25, 227–28, 228–31, 235–36, 302, 307–8, and 313–14.

33 In the absence of a comprehensive first-line index of Jacobean and Caroline poetry, I have been forced to limit my attempts at identification of individual anonymous poems to Crum's *First-Line Index*. A check of the handwritten first-line index at the British Library would, no doubt, make it possible to identify more items than I was able to, but I am sure that many of the pieces in this anthology will remain anonymous because of the nature of ephemeral poetic composition and the practice, in manuscript collections, of ascribing only some of the pieces to known writers.

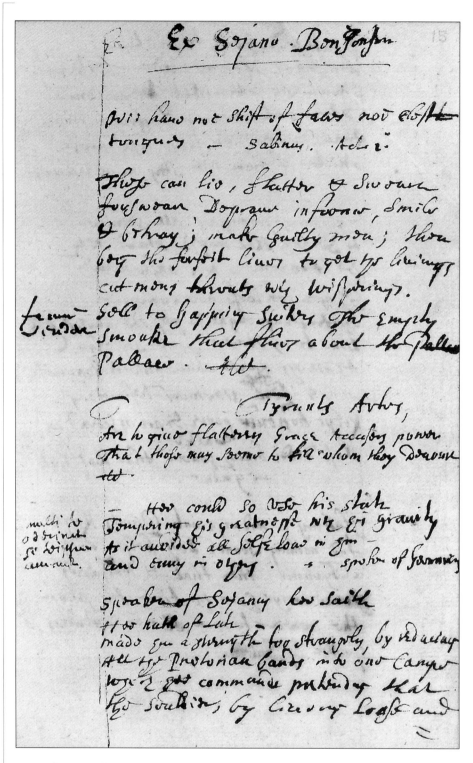

A page from A Collection of Proverbs, Apothegms . . . , Manuscript, ca. 1650 (cat. no. 12).

Folger MS V.a. 263 is described in the Library catalogue as "A collection of proverbs, apothegms … ca. 1650." It is one of many commonplace books from the sixteenth and seventeenth centuries in the manuscript collection. The Maggs Bros. sale catalogue of 1925 from which Henry Clay Folger purchased the manuscript advertised it as a "commonplace book of a seventeenth century student, extending to 307 pp." and emphasized its special interest on account of a long extract from Ben Jonson's tragedy, *Sejanus*, in which "William Shakespeare was one of the principal actors." Doubtless it attracted the attention of Mr. Folger for just such a reason.

The practice of keeping a commonplace book was widespread in early modern England; indeed, it was recommended by all the leading educational theorists of Renaissance humanism—e.g. Erasmus, Vives, Bacon—and prescribed by most grammar school masters and tutors. The purpose of commonplacing was to build up a storehouse of wisdom and Christian virtue through the process of extracting passages from a student's reading, organized under headings such as 'Friendship' or 'Faith.' Scholars have rightly analyzed commonplacing as an ideological as well as a pedagogical practice, describing the extracts annotated as "building blocks of common knowledge and thus basic elements of social cohesion."[1]

At first glance the Folger manuscript may appear to be just such a familiar text. Certainly the volume, as is typical of the genre, consists of a number of extracts—proverbs, adages, and emblems—many of them repeated and glossed by reference to other works, historical examples, and the lives of famous figures. Accordingly the author annotates the emblem *Cunctatio prodest*, illustrated by the mulberry tree (fol. 129v), with reference to Fabius Maximus who was famous for his deliberation. The 'student' of the Folger commonplace book not only arranges proverbs "backed with examples," he evidently had other collections of adages indexed for convenience.[2] Moreover, MS V.a. 263 evidences the *raison d'être* of commonplacing: self-instruction. On the front board of the calf-bound octavo the owner has instructed himself to write the choicest adages next to twenty words.

If the format of the book and the method of glossing the adages appears familiar, the exegetical practice is beyond surprising: it is shocking. Far from the traditional virtues of Christian humanism, the extracts copied and re-copied are resolutely cynical, indeed amoral in tone. The heart of man is always deceitful, the compiler records; by mutual lies men dispatch their business; accordingly, a so-called friend should be treated as an enemy. For, the gloss continues, "vita nostra est militia"—our life is a warfare—and in such a war one should "presuppose the ingratitude and faithlessness of friends" as much as the "envy of neighbours and the fraud and force of enemies."[3] Any expectation we might have that our commonplacer looked traditionally to virtuous governors to rectify the vices of selfish subjects is quickly quashed by a startlingly amoral catalogue of adages and proverbs about public life. The writer regularly repeats aphorisms such as "he who knows not how to dissimulate knows not how to rule," and recommends that unjust acts of power are better dissembled than acknowledged or atoned for.[4] Citing advice that princes should imitate the stealthy wolf and the wily fox as well as the strong lion, the writer also copies a maxim which flies in the face of all the contemporary literature of politics: "a bad man may make a good king."[5]

Such statements, copied and glossed seemingly with no disapproval, evoke a figure who, in urging the prince to imitate the lion and the fox, subverted the moral foundations of Renaissance politics and religion, Niccolò Machiavelli, 'Old Nick.' The Folger commonplacer, as well as invoking the Florentine's counsel to seize every opportunity and to divide and rule, cites Machiavelli as the source of the advice to rulers to deploy fear as an instrument of government; and he annotates his transcription of Machiavelli's *Discourses on Livy* with further examples of rulers' pursuit of interest by subtlety and artifice. Not only are Machiavellian injunctions repeated throughout the commonplace book, but the annotator's personal gloss on his reading appears to be written in the ink of Machiavellian values.

The historical figure our commonplacer most invokes to illustrate wise proverbs in practice is Louis XI, whom he clearly admires as "a great imitator of the subtle prince in all his actions."[6] The other writers he cites, such as Tacitus, Comines, and Cardano, Guicciardini and Bacon, were all seen to be apologists for realpolitik. And even when our commentator refers to texts which exemplify more traditional moral codes—Aristotle, Socrates, and Plutarch, for example—he seems to make them serve a different turn, rendering Aristotle an apologist for raw cunning and Plutarch an advocate of fear as a device of rule. Indeed, in this commonplace book even Scripture is used to teach Machiavellian lessons, the Apostles being cited as support for the view that life was a warfare and Herod taken as a fitting illustration of the efficacy of fear as a mode of government.[7] What we discern, in other words, is a commonplacer who not only read to extract the wisdom of others but one who read to construct a world view and, beyond that, one who brought to his texts and found reinforced by them a pragmatic, utilitarian, and amoral stance on private, social, and public affairs.

It is in this context, rather than Shakespeare's acting history, that we should consider the extensive notes from *Sejanus*. Ben Jonson had freely adapted his source in Tacitus to stage an examination of Machiavellian politics in the court of the Emperor Tiberius and his favorite Aelius Sejanus. The Folger annotator worked carefully through Jonson's text, noting passages on the arts of tyranny and flattery and the use of dissimulation and fear. Sometimes he quoted directly from the play text while in other places he subtly changed Jonson's words into his own idiom, into the language of convenience and necessity. Whatever Jonson's purposes, our commonplacer evidently found in the drama of Tiberius and Sejanus powerful amplification and investigation of the social warfare of human and, especially, political life which he had read in his proverbs and histories.

While other contemporary commonplacers were filling their books with adages exemplifying moral virtue, our annotator had a radically cynical view of the world, with no respect for conventional values and, indeed, still less regard for religion which "makes of men" "excellent fools."[8] We know that, as well as being widely read, he was learned in Latin and Italian, the languages of many of the proverbs. We know too, from his comments and illustrations, that he had a knowledge of recent English history and politics and of favorites such as Robert Carr, first earl of Somerset, and George Villiers, first duke of Buckingham.[9] Most importantly, we know that he was reading and taking notes during the 1650s by his references to Thomas Hobbes's *Leviathan* (fol. 42r) and John Rushworth's *Historical Collections* (fol. 64v), books published in 1651 and 1659 respectively. Beyond that, at least from the manuscript itself, we know nothing of the unusual 'student' who compiled it.

We have direct evidence, however, of the nature of his reading and extracting. On fol. 74v of his commonplace book, commenting on Tiberius's covering his evil designs with "the cloak of religion and liberty," the annotator cross refers to the "Duke of Rohan." As it happens, the Folger Library's copy of Henri, duc de Rohan's *Treatise of the Interest of the Princes and States of Christendome* (London, 1641) is extensively annotated with marginal comment—in the same hand as the commonplace book. Rohan's *Treatise* surveys the various countries and powers of contemporary Europe and analyzes and assesses the "standing of the present affairs" and what "hath caused the ruine of some, or the greatnesse of others."[10] The tone of the treatise is pragmatic and the observations made and lessons drawn are those of a commentator immersed in the realpolitik of the age of the Thirty Years' War. It will come as no surprise, therefore, that the Folger annotator was attracted to the text and subjected it to his own close reading and comment. The theme of interest dominates the manuscript underlinings and annotations of the reader (which we find on almost every page) as well as the authorial printed book. Indeed, the Folger commonplacer makes his own headings such as "maxims of interest observed," "errors committed against interest," and "princes observing their interest" and concludes towards the end of his reading: "men do not only not gain but lose their estates by neglect of their interest." And here, in accordance with the notes describing life as a war, the reader of Rohan doubts not that "every one seeks his own advancement . . . which depends ordinarily upon the destruction of another."[11]

Our reader also brings onto the pages of Rohan's *Treatise* the cross references to other texts that he deployed to explicate proverbs. Along with citations of Tacitus, Malvezzi's commentary on Tacitus, Campanella, the historian Sir Robert Cotton, and Francis Bacon, the authors he most frequently cites are Guicciardini and Machiavelli (both *The Prince* and *The Discourses*). Such cross referencing evidently had a purpose: the extricating of lessons from the fortunes of states and princes, or, as a note on the title page of Rohan's treatise puts it: "'tis good to observe the arts and errors in great states and to consider what were the events of each." Indeed, our annotator flushed out many of Rohan's buried lessons formulating them as maxims. Such maxims are flagged in the margin with the marker "Sen," for "sentence,"[12] and indexed, suggesting that they were to be copied into another commonplace book of adages—perhaps that one referred to in the Folger notebook. The lessons that our annotator observed and proverbialized were not simply those of Rohan's text. This reader had his own contribution to make and deployed Rohan as a place for reflecting on related affairs, noting, for example, on a blank page of the printed book his own "Points of Interest"—among them the arts of dexterity in negotiations and the need to check the greatness of neighbors. Other marginal notes comment, where Rohan does not, on the "admirable prudence" of the Venetians in refusing the Turks' aid against the Papacy, on the reasons for Gustavus Adolphus's entering the war in Germany, and on the folly of the king of Spain "first straining his power so much and after let[ting] it down too low." Our reader has clearly used Rohan for his own meditation on "the causes of the advantages of the world."[13]

The marginalia offer no clear points to the identity of the hand behind them. They suggest a breadth of reading in several languages; and we have a date, for on p. 91 he writes, "they this instant year 1645 in their treaty at Munster endeavour to make the Duke of Bavaria an elector." If our annotator was reading attentively in 1645 and, as the reference to Rushworth indicates, still doing so in 1659, he was clearly a 'student' of affairs long beyond any normal, formal program of school or university education. The wide reading suggests an older man rather than an adolescent, as too the interest in pragmatic politics points to a man of the world rather than an academic. Beyond that, though their author may elude us, what we can conclude from the two Folger documents more generally and importantly is that this early modern reader, far from following the pedagogic prescriptions of the humanist educational program, studied for his own use, to formulate his own codes for a world he perceived as deceitful, vicious, and violent.

There I would probably have left the Folger documents and their author. As it happened, however, I arrived at the Folger after encountering our annotator in four other places, six thousand miles apart. While I was beginning research on a study of representations of authority and images of power at the Huntington Library in 1993, they purchased from Phillips of London what was described in the sale catalogue as a "major new seventeenth century diary," the "autograph journal of Sir William Drake, scholar and manuscript collector, member of the Long Parliament and associate of the Parliamentarians."[14] The 160-page journal, written from both ends, covered the period from 1631 to 1642. No simple diary, it is a book recording events, some legal cases and conversations, with mementoes of self-admonition and advice and notes on skills to acquire and books to obtain and study. The tone of the entries is pragmatic and utilitarian, sometimes ruthlessly so. Headings to notes like "friendship with many for converse but few for endearment" or "the several uses I may make of men" disclose a chillingly cynical, self-interested approach to society.[15] The same preoccupation with interest and advantage informs Drake's view of courtiers, MPs, and rulers. "The whole world," he writes, "is nothing but deceit, lying and vanity"; the law, he reflects, favours the most powerful not the just; and religion was used most often to dupe men. "Interest and advantage with princes," he observes, "overweighs all other considerations"; "the most crafty, faithless and audacious men are those that rule the world."[16]

Drake's diary is not that of a 'student': born in 1606, he was in his twenties and thirties during the period it covers. Nor is it the text of a scholar. The manuscript is full of records of land transactions, business, and converse with men of affairs from the archbishop of Canterbury to MPs such as John Pym and John Hampden and common lawyers. Moreover, Drake counsels himself "not to study much books of learning for they divert business, . . . and keep one from more useful things."[17] Here the reading he most recommends to himself is in law and 'policy'—statutes and proclamations, books on the jurisdictions of courts, parliamentary journals, and such like. Beyond these, his reading list includes the classic texts of policy and realpolitik—Tacitus, Cardano, Comines, works "profitable for a civil life." We find him referring most frequently to Machiavelli and Guicciardini, "the most judicious of modern authors."[18] Drake's diary, in other words, is the work of a practical and cynical man, a Buckinghamshire gentleman living in early Stuart London, reading and observing in order to equip himself to survive in a competitive world, advance his fortunes, and rise in place.

After encountering him for the first time at the Huntington, I followed Sir William Drake back to England. Here the scale of his program of self-instruction in the ways of the world became abundantly apparent. In the library of University College, London, are volumes of manuscripts from the Drake family house, Shardeloes, in Buckinghamshire; among them are thirty-seven commonplace books of reading notes, fifteen in Sir William's hand, the rest in that of a scribe. In addition, I found two other notebooks by him, unidentified, in the Buckinghamshire Record Office and the House of Lords Record Office, along with other printed books with marginalia in his hand. All the holograph manuscripts (and indeed those in the scribal hand) contain notes in English, Italian, Latin, and French from classical and humanist texts and commentaries, notably histories and works of policy, books of adages and proverbs, fables and emblems. In all of them Drake meditates on the extracts he notes, glosses with reference to other works, illustrates axioms from historical examples and characters, and distills the practical lesson (moral would be an inappropriate term) from an event, life, or adage. The notes are the record of a man who, as Stuart Clark observed, "set out to acquire an arsenal of sententious materials,"[19] and they are dominated by the writings of Machiavelli and Guicciardini, the Florentines who were anathematized as very devils subverting all Christian morality and virtuous government.

William Drake penned the Folger commonplace notes and the marginalia in the duke of Rohan's *Treatise*. Drake was not, however, as the Maggs cataloguer believed, a student. He was in his forties and fifties when he made these notes. Born to godly parents, he was tutored by Dr. Charles Croke before going up to Christ Church, Oxford, in 1624. In 1626 he proceeded to the Middle Temple, where he was bound with Sir Simonds D'Ewes, and went on, it seems, to some legal practice. Though he consolidated his Buckinghamshire estates with the purchase of the manor of Amersham, Drake also had property and lived much of the time in London. In the 1630s he traveled to France and the Low Countries. He was elected to Parliament in April 1640 and in 1641 was made a baronet. He was appointed a member of the Parliamentary Association for Buckinghamshire but, soon after the outbreak of civil war, he went abroad and, except for brief periods, did not return until the Restoration when he again sat in Parliament until his death in 1669. That is all we know about the facts of his life. Although a speech by Drake, supposedly to the Long Parliament, was published, we have no independent evidence that it was delivered, and he has left almost no trace in the public records of the years of personal rule, civil war, and interregnum.

Drake's lack of public prominence makes his numerous volumes of commonplace books, if anything, all the more interesting and valuable. For here we may eavesdrop on a gentleman on the fringes of court society, conversing with men of affairs, and weighing experience with his reading and re-reading. The unusual number and the radically amoral tone of his notebooks must lead us to ask why he kept them. We can discount the normal reason—humanist education and scholarship for, as we have seen, Drake had little time for contemplative study. The notes were, as he constantly indicates, for use, to equip him with life skills needed to survive and thrive in the competitive and self-interested society and polity of early Stuart England, which was far removed from the ideals of harmony and cooperation it celebrated. From time to time, evidently, he returned to look over his notes and to add new reflection. Whether he achieved his goals is not clear. He inherited and amassed a considerable estate and purchased a reversion to an office; but whether he harbored higher ambitions remains uncertain. What is certain, and revealing, are his perceptions of the men who governed England from the age of Queen Elizabeth to the Restoration, and his analysis of society, religion, and government.

William Drake's notebooks demonstrate how a gentleman with a conventional upbringing and education could, and did, principally through his own reading, formulate values and beliefs radically at odds with the official scripts and teachings of his age. Of course he prompts us to wonder whether there were others like him—not only his circle of acquaintances who appear to have shared with him his cynical world-view as well as books, but others who, also through a dialogue between reading and experience, constructed personal codes and social and political ideas far removed from our assumptions about the early modern mentalité. Men like Drake read the great works of political thought from which we still write the history of ideas—Aristotle, Machiavelli, and Hobbes. But Drake's process of constructing a world-view and system of belief was what modern critics would call intertextual, a reading of fables, emblems, and proverbs as much as histories and formal political treatises.

The Folger commonplace book V.a. 263 is not of the "first importance," as the sale catalogue vaunted, on account of Shakespeare's acting in *Sejanus*. It is, however, an unusual volume of notes and reflections on texts and events that manifests both a process of self-fashioning by a citizen and the formulation of independent political thinking. It is a manuscript which should lead scholars to look for political ideas not only in the traditional canonical texts but in such 'uncommon' places.

1   Mary Thomas Crane, *Framing Authority: Sayings, Self, and Society in Sixteenth-Century England* (Princeton, NJ, c1993), 18.

2   Folger Shakespeare Library, Washington, DC, MS V.a. 263, fols. 44, 85, 131; at other end, fol. 6.

3   Ibid., fols. 59, 75; cf. University College, London, Bacon-Tottell (i.e. Odgen) MS 7/8, fol. 162v.

4   MS V.a. 263, fols. 25, 54, 73, 95.

5   Ibid., fol. 12; cf. Ogden MS 7/7, fols. 2v, 77; 7/8, fol. 161v; 7/9, fol. 130v.

6   MS V.a. 263, fol. 53; cf. other end fol. 31.

7   Ibid., fols. 59v, 104, 127.

8   Ibid., 41v, 65, 79v.

9   See Kevin Sharpe, *Reading Revolutions: The Politics of Reading in Early Modern England* (New Haven and London, 2000), 225–35, 328–31.

10   See Sharpe, 262–66, and Henri, duc de Rohan, *A Treatise of the Interest of the Princes and States of Christendome* (London, 1641), Folger call number R1868, sigs. A8r, A9v.

11   Rohan, *Treatise*, sigs. A1r-v, A2r; *The Second Part of The Interest of the Princes and States of Christendome* (London, 1641), 124.

12   Sharpe, 262–63.

13   Ibid., 264; Rohan, *Second Part*, 64, 68, 104.

14   Phillipps sale catalogue, 18 March 1993.

15   Henry E. Huntington Library, San Marino, CA, HM 55603, fol. *27; Ogden MS 7/7, fol. 102.

16   HM 55603, fol. *25.

17   Ibid., fol. *1v.

18   Ibid., front flyleaf, fol. *16v.

19   Stuart Clark, "Wisdom Literature of the Seventeenth Century: A Guide to the Contents of the 'Bacon-Tottel' Commonplace Books. Part 1," *Transactions of the Cambridge Bibliographical Society* 6 (1976): 291–305, at 298.

Etched title page by Wenceslaus Hollar from Sir William Dugdale, *Monasticon Anglicanum sive Pandectae coenobiorum Benedictinorum*, London, Richard Hodgkinson, 1655–1673. Folger call no. 152273.

Posh Print and the Polemicization of William Dugdale's *Monasticon Anglicanum* (1655)
Jennifer Andersen

Although William Dugdale deprecated the pamphlets filling the Stationers' stalls during the 1640s and 1650s, he gingerly entered the polemical arena of the times himself through the obscure royalist iconography depicted in the frontispiece of his great antiquarian work, the *Monasticon Anglicanum*. Through historical allusions and emblems, a magnificent etched title page by Wenceslaus Hollar signaled to readers a Laudian commitment to reconstructing traditional church fabrics, a growing tolerance for Catholicism, and opposition to Puritans— all antithetical to the civil war and interregnum periods.

Architectural frontispieces had their origins in humanistic and antiquarian research. The main features of such title pages were an arch, or pediment, flanking columns, and a base, or plinth, enclosing a title written in the fashion of a Roman inscription. This design was based on actual ancient inscriptions sketched by antiquaries. Although they were first used in the manuscripts of Italian humanists, architectural title pages began to be used by publishers and printers throughout Europe in the sixteenth century. Eventually the edifices represented on these title pages served as a scaffolding for a network of complex allusions to the patron, the author, and the contexts of the text. Emblematic title pages spread rapidly throughout Europe due to the flourishing book trade. In the 1520s German Lutherans had first seized on the emblematic title page as pictorial propaganda for reform-minded readers; the title pages to Coverdale's Bible (1535) and the Great Bible (1539) were the earliest examples in England.[1]

In adopting an architectural frontispiece with its framework for historical and symbolic tableaux, Dugdale drew on a design that conveyed both scholarly and polemical implications to readers. There are several levels of meaning and allusion in the *Monasticon* frontispiece. It is framed by a broken arch without a keystone, symbolic of the Interregnum, the state without a king. Three principal scenes capture the reader's attention: the scene at the top of the arch, and the scenes at the bottom left and right of the plinth which supports the arch. On a literal level, these scenes depict pivotal or exemplary moments in the history of English monasticism. The top center compartment shows Henry III confirming Magna Carta to lords spiritual and temporal. Among the spiritual lords are the abbots of the great medieval monasteries.[2] The bottom left compartment shows saintly Edward the Confessor, exemplary patron of the church, kneeling before a triptych. The bottom right compartment shows Henry VIII, despoiler of the Catholic Church in England, brandishing a sword in the air, with ruined monastic buildings in the background.[3] The figures at bottom left and right—pious Edward the Confessor and tyrannical Henry VIII—bracket the history of English monasticism and represent monarchs with polar opposite attitudes toward monasteries. The top center figure of Henry III confirming Magna Carta stands ambiguously under the missing keystone to the arch, representing either the royal power vacuum or crucially holding church and state together.

Another level of meaning in the frontispiece, conveyed by visual and verbal allusions to the works of Dugdale's fellow antiquaries, supplies a narrative of Dugdale's dependence on a network of collective antiquarian endeavors. In very real and material ways, the production of the *Monasticon Anglicanum* depended on a pre-existing body of scholarship, access to collections, and the sharing of transcribed documents. Not only had Sir Henry Spelman, for example, persuaded Roger Dodsworth to accept Dugdale as a collaborator on the *Monasticon*, but he had also arranged access to and sharing of manuscript collections. Dugdale had come to know the history of Henry III (the figure in the top center compartment of his frontispiece) mainly through Sir Robert Cotton's *A Short View of the Long Life and Reigne of Henry the Third* (1642). The figure of Edward the Confessor on the bottom left, as Margery Corbett points out, alludes to an etching which appears on the title page of Lancelot Andrewes's *The Form of Consecration of a Church or Chapel* (1659).[4] The image of Henry VIII relates to a Holbein painting. An allegorical figure of Antiquity in the upper right corner is a personification which appeared on the title page of William Burton's *History of Leicestershire* (1622). And the Anglo-Saxon characters etched into the pillar on the upper right serve as a tribute to Sir Henry Spelman and William Somner, who had studied and translated the Anglo-Saxon texts used in the *Monasticon*.[5] Thus Dugdale also uses the emblematic title page as an opportunity to acknowledge to readers his scholarly debts and influences.

Yet a third level of meaning is typological, in which the historical scenes represent earlier examples of contemporary events. On this level, the figures at bottom left and right are the most transparent: the bottom left figure and the tableau surrounding him echo the engraving of Charles I on the title page of *Eikon Basilike* (1649), and Henry VIII stands for sacrilegious Puritan iconoclasts. The typological significance for Dugdale of Magna Carta's confirmation by Henry III is clarified by a parallel he worked out at length discursively in his *Short View of the Late Troubles in England* (1681). In the final two chapters of that treatise, Dugdale drew historical parallels between the English civil wars, the thirteenth-century Barons' War, and the sixteenth-century French wars of religion. Thus Dugdale saw the medieval English King Henry III as a type for the French King Henry III (killed in the French wars of religion) and for England's Charles I. In Dugdale's view, all of these monarchs were martyred in struggles with rapacious parliaments or nobles who cloaked seditious purposes in the guise of religious reform. Even though the *Short View* was not published until 1681, Dugdale composed it from notebooks which he had kept while with the royal court at Oxford in the 1640s, so we can assume that these historical parallels had already occurred to him at the time the frontispiece to the *Monasticon* was designed.[6] This level of typological allusion in the emblematic frontispiece thus reflects a veiled royalist providentialism. The historical and visual allusions in the title page would probably have been obscure to all but a charmed circle of antiquarian cognoscenti. Such an elitist approach to highly encoded polemical messages was typical of royalist propaganda and in keeping with the belief that the mysteries of state, the *arcana imperii*, should be revealed to the king and his qualified inner circle of counselors alone.[7] They were not aimed at a wide audience of general readers.

The royalist and Laudian sympathies on display in the title page may have made the *Monasticon* a politically volatile item at the time of its publication.[8] To be sure, the text itself was not polemical, consisting mostly of transcriptions of manuscript monastic charters and of land endowments written in Latin. But it was feared by some that those land titles could be used to support the return of monastic lands to the church, and thus to aid the attendant return of Roman Catholicism to England. In a marginal note to his copy of the *Life of Dugdale*, Anthony à Wood derisively dismisses the suspicion of a crypto-papist subtext to the *Monasticon*:

> Here it will not (I presume) be amisse to take notice, that whereas since his Majesty's happy restoration, some persons of note, who were in great place and power in the time of the late usurpation, and as yet are no small countenancers of those separatists, which are again busily endeavoring the ruine of monarchy, to blast and vilifye this worke of the Monasticons, have maliciously given out, that the designe of making it publique by the presse was purposely to discover the land sometime belonging to the religious houses in this realme; to the intent that upon restoreing the Romish religion, which they would have it believed is much feigned, they might returne to their former superstitious uses. – I shall therefore here make a briefe digression, cleerly to manyfest the falseness and absurdity of that suggestion, by three irrefragable instances. The first is, that a cheife promoter of the worke was the late Lord Fairfax, the Parliament's Generall in theire bloudy wars against the King, (whom none of that party did every suspect to be popishly affected), allowing Mr. Roger Dodsworth 40 l. per annum during his life for his support therein, as is very well knowne: and that Mr. John Rushworth (then his secretary) through the influence he at that time had upon those who kept the records in the Tower of London, procured for the said Mr. Dodsworth and Mr. Dugdale free accesse unto them, with liberty to make transcripts of whatsoever did relate to this collection without payment of any fees . . . .[9]

Even though Wood refutes the charge of crypto-catholicism, his note confirms that such a perception existed. Although the *Monasticon* was not used to restore monasteries to the Roman Catholic Church, eventually it was invoked in disputes over titles to land in support of the interests of landed gentry families granted dissolved monastic lands by Parliament under Henry VIII. It is no surprise that there should have been apprehension during the Interregnum about making accessible in print over a thousand pages of ancient land endowments because the sequestration and sale of crown, church, and royalist lands during the civil wars gave a new charge to ancient charters like those transcribed in the *Monasticon Anglicanum*. The archbishop of York, for example, had been declared a delinquent and his estates sequestered and turned to other uses by Parliament in 1643. After episcopacy was abolished in 1646, the way was cleared for the sale of episcopal lands to help finance the war.[10] Thus Parliamentarians might well fear reprisals for the taxation and sale of royalist lands during the war. There is some evidence that the *Monasticon* was used in settling Restoration land disputes: a 1668 letter from James Milner to John Rogers of Gunby, Yorkshire, mentions that the *Monasticon Anglicanum* was sometimes given in evidence at the Assizes.[11] In 1693 an abridged English translation of the *Monasticon* was published which made it more portable and accessible to more readers. It was advertised by Joseph Wright as a "Restoration tax-evader's guide."[12] So while anti-popish fears that the *Monasticon* would provide legal support for the return of monastic lands to the Roman Catholic Church turned out to be unfounded, some readers did invoke the *Monasticon* as a semi-legal document in land disputes.

Dugdale took advantage of the title page design to send a coded royalist message to readers, but the principal patron of the project, as Wood pointed out, had in fact been none other than Sir Thomas Fairfax, Lord General of the parliamentary army. To explain this apparent ideological incongruity, we must look back almost forty years to the origins of the project, well before it was printed. Although Dugdale was primarily responsible for seeing the *Monasticon* into print in the 1650s and his name primarily has become attached to it, he was not the principal compiler of the volume.[13] The *Monasticon's* production begins more properly with Roger Dodsworth (1585–1654), a Yorkshire antiquary patronized by the Fairfax family of that county, who had been gathering materials for a history of Yorkshire monasteries (a *Monasticon Boreale*) since 1618. Dodsworth's transcriptions of manuscript charters and endowments soon extended to other northern counties, and when in 1638 he met William Dugdale (1605–1686), a younger Warwickshire antiquary, the two agreed to pool their data into a comprehensive history of monasteries in England, the *Monasticon Anglicanum*.

The plan to collaborate was somewhat deferred in the suspended reality of the civil war and interregnum. Both continued to copy monastic documents wherever they could gain access to them, and ironically, the fact that each had a major patron on opposing sides of the royalist-parliamentarian divide allowed them optimal access to major English libraries. Dugdale remained with the royal court at Oxford and other royalist strongholds from 1642 to 1646; he traveled briefly to France with his royalist patron Sir Christopher Hatton; and he spent the remainder of the 1640s on his sequestered estate of Blythe Hall under a form of house arrest. At Oxford he continued his researches at the Bodleian Library, and the libraries of Christ Church and Magdalen Colleges; in France he compared research with French monastic antiquarians; and his forced stay at Blythe Hall gave him the uninterrupted time he needed to write his *Antiquities of Warwickshire* (1656). Dodsworth, meanwhile, obtained access to records in the Tower of London, the State Paper Office, and York Castle through his patron Fairfax, Lord General of the New Model Army from 1645, and Fairfax's secretary, John Rushworth, also Dodsworth's cousin and another antiquarian enthusiast.[14]

By 1648 Dodsworth and Dugdale renewed their collaboration, sharing and comparing copies and transcripts of documents. Though their manuscript was ready for the press in 1651, the difficulty of finding a publisher delayed its printing until 1655, a year after Dodsworth's death. In a letter from 20 August 1651 to his friend William Vernon, Dugdale laments the difficulty of finding a publisher:

> Sr, As for Mr. Dodsworths workes they are great, and cannot come to maturitye
> very quickly. His worke of Monasterye foundations is ready for ye Presse, if ye
> times were such as they have bin, to vend it in case it were printed, but I neede
> not tell you how learninge growes to a lower ebbe every day more then other, nor
> in what condition the cheife patrons and lovers of it are: therefore 'tis noe wonder
> if little else but Pamphlets now fill ye Stationers stalls.[15]

In the end, Dodsworth advanced a fairly large sum toward the printing of the first volume, and he and Dugdale filled out the balance with joint loans. When Dodsworth died in 1654, the task of assembling and editing material, seeing it through the press, and supervising the illustrations fell to Dugdale. One way he cut costs was by publishing the massive work serially in three volumes over the course of almost twenty years. The most expensive part of the book was the engravings, and Dugdale's correspondence reveals that some individual plates were paid for by families whose arms or ancestral lands were depicted in them. Upon seeing a pre-publication copy of the *Monasticon Anglicanum* in 1655, for example, Sir Edward Walker, Dugdale's predecessor in the College of Heralds, offered "in despite of the low and retired condition I am reduced unto . . . to give a Print of the Remaines of that Abby and Church, if there bee any to bee inserted in ye Worke" and to employ his "old friend" Wenceslaus Hollar to engrave it.[16] Eventually many plates were sponsored by aristocratic donors who paid £5 towards the cost and in return had their names, family arms, and mottoes inscribed on the plates they funded. Despite the high cost of producing the plates, all three volumes of the *Monasticon* sold used for £7-£8 in the late-seventeenth century. Unfortunately, only ten of the sixty-nine plates that appeared in the first volume of *Monasticon Anglicanum* were the correct and delicate work of the masterful Wenceslaus Hollar. Most others were engraved by the comparative amateur Daniel King, apparently patronized by Lord Fairfax, who must have recommended King to Dodsworth, another Yorkshire retainer.[17]

The final product of Dodsworth's antiquarian labors bears no trace of Fairfax's role as chief sponsor of the project. Dodsworth had received an annual pension from the Fairfax family, which was promised to continue for three years after his death to finance the publication of the *Monasticon*. Dodsworth wanted the book to be dedicated to Lord Fairfax and suggested that Dugdale write the dedication, but no such acknowledgment appears in the volume. Anthony à Wood's reference to Fairfax as the book's chief promoter suggests that his patronage was well known, at least in antiquarian circles. Fairfax may have withdrawn from a highly visible role in the project because his association with it opened him up to suspicions of royalist and Laudian tendencies (the direction it had taken in Dugdale's hands) at a time when, having retired from the generalship of the parliamentary army, Fairfax was attempting to remain politically neutral.

By the time of the *Monasticon*'s publication, the implications of Dodsworth's and Dugdale's research had become political in ways that neither could have anticipated. A work that started as an expression of local county pride, as it lumbered into being over the course of the seventeenth century, had come to bristle with significance for political, religious, and social controversies of the day. The resonances of monastic history with contemporary events reverberate especially in the book's emblematic title page, where Dugdale seems ultimately to have recognized the book's publication as a polemical opportunity for appealing to royalist readers.[18] While Richard Helgerson lumps Dugdale together with other seventeenth-century antiquaries, suggesting that their chorography had anti-monarchical, Whiggish implications, Dugdale's *Monasticon* vividly illustrates potential royalist and clericalist tendencies in antiquarian research.[19] Its cryptic frontispiece, Latin text, legal charters, and aristocratic sponsorship indicate that it was, from start to finish, intended for an elite audience of intellectuals or landed gentry who could read between the lines.

1   See Margery Corbett and Ronald Lightbown, *The Comely Frontispiece: the Emblematic Title-Page in England 1550–1660* (London, 1979), 8–9; Margery Corbett, "The Architectural Title-Page: an attempt to trace its development from its Humanist origins up to the sixteenth and seventeenth centuries, to the heyday of the complex engraved title-page," *Motif* 12 (1964): 48–62.

2   This scene of the confirmation of Magna Carta by Henry III lists a reference to the thirteenth-century monastic historian Matthew Paris ("vide Matt. Paris Pag. 866"), referring to another folio that had been printed in 1640 by Richard Hodgkinson, the printer of the first volume of the *Monasticon Anglicanum*. The medieval Latin language, the subject matter, and the format of this 1640 edition of Paris's *Historia Major* would have recommended Hodgkinson as competent to print a work like the *Monasticon*.

3   On Renaissance nostalgia triggered by medieval ruins see Margaret Aston, "English Ruins and English History: the Dissolution and the Sense of the Past," *Journal of the Warburg and Courtauld Institutes* 36 (1973): 231–55.

4   Margery Corbett deciphers the complex language of historical reference, allegorical figure, and visual allusion in Hollar's title page extensively in "The Title-Page and Illustrations of the *Monasticon Anglicanum,* 1655–1673," *The Antiquaries Journal* 67 (1987): 102–10. H. A. Cronne discusses affinities between the work of Spelman and Dugdale in "The Study and Use of Charters by English Scholars in the Seventeenth Century: Sir Henry Spelman and Sir William Dugdale" in *English Historical Scholarship in the Sixteenth and Seventeenth Centuries,* Levi Fox, ed. (London, 1956), 73–92.

5   Some of these allusions are discussed by Corbett, "Title-Page and Illustrations," 107–8.

6   The full title, as typographically rendered in the first edition, is: *A SHORT VIEW OF THE LATE TROUBLES IN ENGLAND; Briefly setting forth, Their Rise, Growth, and Tragical Conclusion. As also, some Parallel thereof with the Barons-Wars in the time of King Henry III. But chiefly with that in France, called the HOLY LEAGUE, in the Reign of Henry III. And Henry IV. Late Kings of that Realm* (London, 1681). Philip Styles contrasts an early manuscript draft of the *Late Troubles* with the printed version in "Dugdale and the Civil War," *Birmingham and Warwickshire Archaeological Society Transactions* 86 (1974): 132–44.

7   On royalist uses of propaganda, see Tim Harris, "Propaganda and Public Opinion in Seventeenth-Century England," in *Media and Revolution: Comparative Perspectives*, Jeremy Popkin, ed. (Lexington, KY, 1995), 57–59.

8   A contemporary case in which an engraving was judged seditious is recorded in the 1651 bill of indictment against the printmaker Robert Vaughan for engraving a portrait of Prince Charles with the aim of promoting the royal heir. What perhaps distinguished this case from the *Monasticon* engraving was an inscription proclaiming Charles to be king which accompanied the Vaughan engraving. See *Middlesex County Records* ed. John Cory Jefferson (1888), vol. III: 205–7, 286, 287.

9   Printed in *The Life, Diary, and Correspondence of Sir William Dugdale, Knight, Sometime Garter Principal King of Arms*, ed. William Hamper, (London, 1827), 25. I must thank Laetitia Yeandle for helping me track down the location of Wood's copy to Mss. Wood 8492 in F. Madan, H. H. E. Craster, N. Denholm-Young, *A Summary Catalogue of Western Manuscripts in the Bodleian Library at Oxford*, vol. II, part II (Oxford, 1937). The fact that Wood himself was suspected of popery upon the publication of his life work, the *Athenae Oxoniensis*, may have predisposed him to sympathize with Dugdale; see Sabrina Baron's entry on Anthony à Wood in the *Dictionary of Literary Biography*.

10 I. J. Gentles and W. J. Sheils, *Confiscation and Restoration: The Archbishopric Estates and the Civil War* (York: Borthwick Papers No. 59, 1981). See also H. J. Habakkuk, "Public Finance and the Sale of Confiscated Property during the Interregnum," *Economic History Review* 15 (1962): 70–88; H. E. Chesney, "The Transference of Lands in England, 1640–1660," *Transactions of the Royal Historical Society*, 4th series, 15 (1932): 181–210; and Joan Thirsk, "The Restoration Land Settlement," *Journal of Modern History* 26 (1954): 315–28.

11 This letter is at the Leeds Central Library; it is mentioned in Francis Maddison, Dorothy Styles, Anthony Wood, *Sir William Dugdale 1605–1686: A List of His Printed Works and of His Portraits with Notes on His Life and the Manuscript Sources* (Warwick, 1953), 84.

12 See Graham Parry, *The Trophies of Time: English Antiquarians of the Seventeenth Century* (Oxford, 1995), 230.

13 D. C. Douglas's chapter on Dugdale entitled "The Grand Plagiary" recaps the allegation that the material for the first and second volumes of the *Monasticon* was largely collected and written by Dodsworth; see *English Scholars* (London, 1939), 31–59. The first and second volumes had Dodsworth's and Dugdale's names on the title page, but the third volume bears only Dugdale's name, and it may be from this that the whole work has come to be known as Dugdale's.

14 Information about Dodsworth is taken from the *Dictionary of National Biography* and N. Denholm-Young and H. H. E. Craster, "Roger Dodsworth (1585–1564) and His Circle," *Yorkshire Archaeological Journal* 32 (1934): 5–32. Denholm-Young and Craster reconstruct a detailed chronology of Dodsworth's research activities from 1605 to 1652 from his notebooks, 17–32. Surviving correspondence between Dodsworth and Dudgale is printed in Hamper, *Life* (1827), 226–31, 233–37, 253–55.

15 This letter is printed in Hamper, *Life*, 263–64. Dugdale used a similar method of financing the publication of his *Antiquities of Warwickshire* (1656) by obtaining subscriptions for including heralds' pedigrees of gentry families. In the preface, he lists families whose pedigrees he omitted because their present heads would not contribute to the costs of publication, plus those whom he would have left out had he known they would not pay up.

16 This letter is printed in Hamper, *Life*, 293.

17 See Rachel Doggett, Julie Biggs, Carol Brobeck, *Impressions of Wenceslaus Hollar* (Washington, DC, 1996), 41; Voet auction catalog, cat. no. 40, fols. 43v–44v. I am grateful to Sabrina Baron for this reference.

18 See F. Smith Fussner, *The Historical Revolution: English Historical Writing and Thought 1580–1640* (London, 1962).

19 Richard Helgerson, "The Land Speaks," in *Forms of Nationhood: The Elizabethan Writing of England* (Chicago, IL, 1992), 107–47. Ann Hughes offers a much more satisfactory account of the motives behind the gentry's interest in antiquarianism, and in particular of the circle of Warwickshire antiquarians to which Dugdale belonged, in *Politics, Society and Civil War in Warwickshire, 1620-1660* (Cambridge, 1987), 47–50.

"To Conclude Aright Within Ourselves":

Narcissus Luttrell and the Burden of the Protestant Reader, 1678–88

Anna Battigelli

Few early modern readers read more assiduously or more methodically than the annalist and antiquary Narcissus Luttrell (1657–1732). By nature reserved, Luttrell nevertheless followed print controversy avidly, even compulsively. Around the time of the Popish Plot, when he was twenty-one, he established three lifetime habits that absorbed his waking hours and shaped his predominantly textual adult experience. The first of these is well known: he acquired ephemera, usually inscribing the date of publication in the upper left-hand corner of a piece's title page.[1] To the publication date, he frequently also noted the price he paid for the item, or "gratis" when he was not charged. His practice seems to have been to bind material together by topic, arranging items within a volume by publication date.[2] Although his collection was eventually dispersed, his neat, recognizable handwriting and methodical consistency in dating items allow scholars to identify items from his collection. Today, thanks to the industry of James Marshall Osborn and Stephen Parks, 3,405 items have been identified as formerly owned by Luttrell, and this list is still growing.[3]

The second of his habits is also known: he compiled lengthy annals of his times, though he seems not to have intended to publish these.[4] The six-volume *A Brief Historical Relation of State Affairs from September 1678 to April 1714* was only published in 1857, after Thomas Babington Macaulay called attention to it by citing it in *The History of England* (1848–1861). Like the parliamentary diary that Luttrell kept between 1691 and 1693, which was not published until 1972, *A Brief Relation* testifies to Luttrell's interest in recording current events as they unfolded. Proclamations, addresses, petitions, executions, fires, weather, printers' legal troubles, and evidence of popish conspiracies and fanatic counter-conspiracies are the kinds of items and events documented in *A Brief Relation*. Until recently historians have viewed Luttrell's reliance on contemporary newspapers as a liability: the entry in the *Dictionary of National Biography* discusses *A Brief Relation* by noting that "although valuable, many of Luttrell's notes are excerpts from contemporary newspapers, and the many confusions in dates by which the work is characterized are due either to errors in the newspapers, or to their dates of issue being accepted by Luttrell as the dates of the events recorded in them." Today, however, Luttrell's attention to the reality created by print culture's circulation of news, rumor, and gossip makes his work interesting to historians studying early modern habits of reading.

The last habit, the focus of this essay, has not been discussed in print, though it is intimately linked to the first two habits: Luttrell kept commonplace books, blank volumes into which he paraphrased or quoted passages from his reading followed by a brief and

RELIGIO LAICI

OR A

Laymans Faith.

A

POEM.

Atheisticall.

Written by Mr. *DRYDEN.*

Ornari res ipfa negat ; contenta doceri.

LONDON,

Printed for *Jacob Tonfon* at the *Judge's Head* in
Chancery-lane, near *Fleet-ſtreet.* 1682.
28 Nov.

Title page from Narcissus Luttrell's copy of John Dryden, *Religio Laici, or a Laymans Faith*, London, 1682. Folger call no. Wing D2342a copy 2.

often approximate title, page number, and date of publication. At least seven of these reading notebooks exist.[5] Each volume typically focuses on a particular controversy or text. One, for example, served him as he read through the Bible; another, as he read through the polemic surrounding the revocation of the Edict of Nantes.[6] That he kept more than one commonplace book going at once is suggested by the fact that citations to the same work appear in more than one commonplace book. Punctilious by nature, he often prepared a blank index at the back of each volume by neatly dividing pages into four blocks, each block allowing for entries under a particular letter of the alphabet to be added as Luttrell discovered passages in his reading that he considered worthy of entering into his notebooks.

These three activities—collecting, chronicling, and commonplacing—naturally complemented one another: as he collected and arranged material for binding, he compiled annals of his time and used his commonplace books to synthesize and sift through his reading—not necessarily in that order. Insofar as the reality created by the texts he read became more urgent for him than any other reality, Luttrell's reading habits reflect the degree to which the printed word played an increasingly important role in political events in the period following the English civil wars, and particularly during the years straddled by the Popish Plot and the Glorious Revolution.[7] It is not coincidental that Luttrell's reading, collecting, and excerpting began in earnest with the allegations of a Popish Plot to assassinate the king in September 1678, allegations that quickly took on a reality of their own through frenzied printed accounts of plots and counter-plots. The first entry of *A Brief Relation* focuses on the revelation of the Popish Plot:

> September 1678: About the latter end of this month was a hellish conspiracy, contrived and carried on by the papists, discovered by one Titus Oates unto sir Edmondbury Godfrey, justice of the peace, who took his examination on oath.

The entries for 1678–1689 in *A Brief Relation* reveal Luttrell keeping a wary eye on the domestic instability threatened by real and imagined conspiracies and by reports of increasing French persecution of the Huguenots.

He was not alone in collecting pieces pertaining to the Plot.[8] That others also collected such material is reflected in the fact that catalogues of material about the Plot were published. Luttrell's annotated copies of two of these catalogues exist, and as James Osborn has noted, they reveal Luttrell's thoroughness as a collector: he succeeded in obtaining copies of all but one of the texts cited in these two extant catalogues.[9] Osborn adds that

> the very fact that these catalogues were compiled and published is of considerable interest in the history of British book collecting. The publisher's purpose was

stated when the three lists were re-issued in 1680 as *A General Catalogue* (Wing G496), where we read on the title-page, "Very useful for Gent. that make Collections." This statement implies that even when the Popish Plot was at its height, enough book collectors were actively accumulating ephemeral publications to encourage the compilation and printing of these catalogues (Osborn, 5).

Luttrell's interest in ephemera, evident in the nature of his collection and in the focus of *A Brief Relation*, is also evident in six of his seven extant commonplace books. It also points to his departure from the standard Renaissance practice of commonplacing. Kevin Sharpe has noted that commonplacing was from the Renaissance through the eighteenth century part of "a normal habit of reading."[10] The typical practice was to inscribe passages from authoritative sources to be used in written and oral school exercises. According to Sharpe:

> The experience of reading for most boys was, it is not too much to say, the practice of commonplacing. . . . As early as the twelfth century, Peter of Blois had defended the habit of excerpting and compiling "from a repeated reading of books" as fostering "the stuff of virtue and the exercise of prudence". Erasmus and his disciples undoubtedly considered the commonplace book an effective means in training young men in virtue, that is in the values of the Christian humanism that he taught.[11]

Quoting Francis Bacon, Sharpe adds that "from the beginning in collecting familiar knowledge, the commonplace book served 'to furnish argument to dispute . . . likewise to minister unto our judgment to conclude aright within ourselves.'" [12]

Like Bacon, Luttrell believed that reading could guide "judgment to conclude aright within ourselves." As one of his entries notes, books offered the reader "a Conversation with the best men of the former ages, an elaborate conversation wherein they discover to us their best thoughts."[13] But it is significant that this excerpt paraphrases not a standard authority from the past but a text published in 1694, Jean de Lacroze's *The History of Learning: Giving a Succinct Account & Narrative of the Choicest New Books: with a Translation of What is Most Curious and Remarkable in Forreign Journals.* Thus, Luttrell departed from Renaissance commonplacing in that his commonplace books, with the exception of one devoted to the Bible, quote not standard authorities but ephemera: sermons, treatises, pamphlets, learning manuals, and catechisms. He read Latin fluently, but he seems to have turned to standard authorities only in response to arguments made by contemporary writers. He was less interested, then, in authoritative sources than he was in up-to-the-minute polemic. As such, Luttrell's commonplace books reveal a shift in the reading public's understanding of authority: rather than locating that authority in the past, Luttrell locates authority in his own judgment as that judgment is informed by contemporary polemic. To "conclude aright" within himself meant keeping up-to-date with printed controversy.

Reading and excerpting ephemera, then, seem to have provided Luttrell with a mechanism for "conclud[ing] aright." As he read through material, he aimed at boiling down arguments to a few sentences so as to absorb them fully. One of his excerpts under the rubric of 'Books' suggests a method for this distillation:

> The best way of answering these [books], is to pick out what is most materiall, which may be done in a little compasse; & that method hath many advantages; it will not require much time in the writing of it, which is necessary for sett discourses, so may be done by those who are in buisy stations; it would not take up much time in the reading of it; the price of it would be small so that any one might purchase it/ Out of a tract in 4° entitled *The Occasional Paper* numb. 1 1696 pag. 5.[14]

By distilling arguments into their most economical form, one could master them and move on. Distilling arguments also helped the polemicist fulfill the obligation to understand an opponent's argument fully. A later entry puts it this way:

> We must be sure to understand another man's thoughts before we undertake to confute him; for unlesse we perceive from what affections or mistakes a mans opinions rise, we can't convince or satisfie him; we must therefore endeavour to enter into our adversaries mind, & suppose ourselves to be in the same circum-stances, to have the same thoughts & affections abt us, yt he had when he writt; thereby following his errors to their beginning, we may find a way to unravel them or show him how he came to be misled.[15]

Thus, Luttrell seems to have considered the entries in his commonplace books as part of the process of disputation: the ultimate aim of recording an opposing point of view was to first master it so as to "confute" it.

All of Luttrell's commonplace books focus on religion, and it is clear that he considered disputation an essential part of his religious sensibility. As one of the passages he cites notes, "To believe without a reason for it, is credulity, not faith."[16] Elsewhere he recorded the claim that "It is the privilege & duty of man to enquire & examine before he believes or judges; & never give up his assent, to any thing, but upon good & rational grounds."[17] Although his larger commonplace books range broadly over problems confronting the pious man—

ambition, zeal, drunkenness—his smaller ones work differently, focusing on a particular controversy as if the very process of compiling a distilled overview of the various and competing points of view helped one attain command of an issue.

If we look at the small commonplace book that Luttrell titled "A Confutation of Popish Errors Collected out of Various Authors," we can observe his efforts at comprehending and coming to terms with competing Anglican and Catholic doctrines. The sixteen items cited in this book were published between 1672 and 1692, thirteen of them between 1685 and 1687. The backdrop to Luttrell's reading seems to have been the growing anxiety regarding Catholicism following two events in 1685: in February, Charles II died, leaving the throne to his Roman Catholic brother, James II; in October, Louis XIV revoked the Edict of Nantes, eliminating what was left of toleration to French Protestants. Anxiety that James's Catholicism would by definition lead to absolutism and perhaps even to the imposition of Catholicism in England was fueled by rumors that the French were persecuting Protestants and forcing them to convert to Catholicism. Luttrell seems to have felt an obligation to understand Catholic dogma: he patiently examined and defined Catholic attitudes toward saints, images, candles, incense, the adoration of the Sacrament, the laying on of hands, and limbo. The first entries record arguments from tracts written by French Catholic apologists like Jacques Bossuet, who not only insisted that no persecution had been used in converting French Protestants, but also that the conversions were the direct result of "the Character of Baptism," which "secretly recall'd" the converts.[18] Luttrell's point of view emerges in his use of the pronouns "they" and "we," which firmly distinguish between the Catholic positions he records and his own position as a member of the Anglican Church.[19] But the tone of his early entries is explorative rather than judgmental: "*They* urge agt *us*, that *we* cannot deny but before the reformation people were sav'd under the ministry of the roman church, & consequently that the true church was there also" [emphasis mine].[20]

This initial exploratory tone changes, however, as Luttrell records passages from a text that, like his commonplace books, purports to represent competing points of view: *A Catechism Truly Representing the Doctrines and Practices of the Church of Rome, with an Answer thereunto. By a Protestant of the Church of England* (London, 1686).[21] Its title appears to suggest a comparison and contrast of Catholic and Anglican doctrines, and in fact the text prints the Catholic catechism on the left page with a corresponding Anglican catechism on the right page. Luttrell declared his fondness for this sort of dialogue elsewhere: "The method of writing by way of dialogue is of all the most pleasing to the reader."[22] But the dialogue that results from the facing catechisms in this text is carefully crafted to serve as a point-by-point refutation of Catholicism. Luttrell's use of this text emerges in an entry remarking on the Catholic Church's use of Latin. The objective of a church service, he notes, should be to "inform the mind, engage the affections & increase devotion; but that cannot be done, where the tongue it is celebrated in is not understood."[23] In succeeding entries, Luttrell continues confuting the Catholic apologists quoted earlier by recording excerpts from Protestant sermons such as William Sherlock's *A Discourse Concerning the Object of Religious Worship* (London, 1685). In this manner, Luttrell's "A Confutation of Popish Errors" serves as a compendium of points of view, but it carefully arranges those points of view so as to arrive at a conclusion that seems to have been planned from the beginning. The penultimate entry quotes from a sermon that presents a traditionally anti-Catholic view of Catholicism as based on the denial of rational inquiry—precisely the opposite of his feeling that "To believe without a reason for it, is credulity, not faith"[24]:

> The church of Rome is a church whose doctrines contradict common sense, the principles of reason, the rules of morality, the known lawes of Christ; a church that magisterially imposes upon mens consciences, makes what new articles of faith it pleaseth, binds under the penalty of damnation to an implicit faith and obedience to all its decrees . . . . a church idolatrous in the worshipping of Images, the adoration of a piece of bread, the invocation of saints & angels & veneration of relicks & crucifixes.[25]

The feelings unleashed in this passage seem to serve as the culmination of Luttrell's implicit argument that the Protestant reliance upon individual reason was superior to the perceived Catholic denial of rational inquiry.

But the title of this commonplace book—"A Confutation of Popish Errors Collected Out of Various Authors"—also suggests the difficulty posed to Luttrell by his immersion in ephemera. His private and careful arrangement of selected excerpts leading to a firm conclusion was, of course, exactly the obverse of what was happening in the literary marketplace, which generated endless permutations of competing points of view. The variety of arguments he records in this book suggests both his confidence in his own individual judgment and the palpable strain that judgment experienced as he sifted through competing points of view. His private and intense interest in excerpting and arranging passages from the broad variety of texts he read, then, points to a crucial aspect of his reading experience. On the one hand, his commonplace books reflect a new understanding of authority by locating that authority in individual judgment as that judgment is informed by contemporary polemic; on the other hand, they also suggest the particular burden placed on the pious Protestant reader by this shifting understanding of the roles of reason and authority. Luttrell's appetite for alternative ways of looking at the world is evident in his broad-ranging and nearly comprehensive collection of ephemera; that same appetite, however, seems to have created a need, perhaps even a compulsion, to order and arrange.

1   James Marshall Osborn established in 1957 that Luttrell's dates referred to the date of publication and not to Luttrell's purchase dates. Phillip Harth has concurred, noting that Osborn "proved beyond any reasonable doubt that what Luttrell had recorded in each case was the date of publication." Stephen Parks similarly agrees. The fact that the dates Luttrell inscribed in his copy of *A Continuation of the Compleat Catalogue of Stitch'd Books . . . since the Discovery of the Popish Plot* and in *A Second Continuation* concur with the anonymous compiler's order in arranging items also suggests that Luttrell noted the date of publication rather than the date of purchase. See James Marshall Osborn, "Reflections on Narcissus Luttrell (1657–1732)," *The Book Collector* (Spring 1957): 3–15 (reprinted in *The Luttrell File*, Stephen Parks, ed. [New Haven, CT, 1999], 3–15); Phillip Harth, *Pen for a Party: Dryden's Tory Propaganda and Its Contexts* (Princeton, NJ, 1993), x; *The Luttrell File*, iii.

2   The Newberry Library owns volumes of poetry that Luttrell collected and arranged chronologically. These items do not seem to be included in Parks's *The Luttrell File*. See shelf marks 6a 158; 6a 159. Sir Walter Scott marveled at Luttrell's ecclecticism in collecting a broad range of poetry: "This industrious collector seems to have bought every poetical tract, of whatever merit, which was hawked through the streets in his time. . . . His collection contains the earliest editions of many of our most excellent poems, bound up, according to the order of the time, with the lowest trash of Grub-Street." *The Works of John Dryden*, ed. Sir Walter Scott (1808); revised and corrected by George Saintsbury I (Edinburgh, 1882), xiii.

3   Stephen Parks, Curator of the James Marshall and Marie-Louise Osborn Collection at Yale University's Beinecke Rare Book and Manuscript Library, has provided a great service in publishing James Osborn's file of items in Luttrell's collection. See *The Luttrell File* cited above.

4   Although Luttrell seems to have been uninterested in publishing his *Brief Historical Relation*, he nevertheless took pains to insure the annal's preservation. In his "Directions Left in Charge to my Wife," he asks that in the event she outlives her son, she see that his books are left to "such of my Relations as will be sure to keep them & make use of them, or to some publick Library, as that at Gray's Inn." See Yale University's Beinecke Rare Book and Manuscript Library, Osborn Shelves C65. Hereafter, all references to the Beinecke's James Marshall and Marie-Louise Osborn Collection will be abbreviated to "Osborn Shelves" followed by the shelf mark.

5   Six of these are in the Beinecke: Osborn MS b 270; Osborn Shelves b 321; Osborn Shelves b269; Osborn Shelves b 47 [3 vols.]. A seventh commonplace book on popish and Protestant controversies, ca. 1687–1715, is in the Folger Shakespeare Library in Washington, DC: Folger MS K.b. 2.

6   The reading notebook Luttrell kept as he read through the Bible is in the Beinecke (Osborn MS b270) as is "A Confutation of Popish Errors Collected out of Various Authors" (Osborn Shelves b 269).

7   Lincoln Faller notes that "beginning with the Interregnum, it can be argued, printing and political life developed in England synergistically; news of all kinds gained a currency and power it had not had before." Faller cites David Ogg, who claims that the power of the printed word reached a highpoint with the Revolution. "Never before," he says, "had the printed word played such a part in political events." See Faller, "King William, 'K.J.,' and James Whitney: The Several Lives and Affiliations of a Jacobite Robber," *Eighteenth-Century Life* 12:3 (1988): 101. See also Ogg, *England in the Reigns of James II and William III* (London, 1969), 222.

8   Luttrell added to and broadened his collection until his death, after which his son Francis, who inherited the collection, continued to add to it. For the purposes of this essay, I focus on the political and religious nature of his collection, but it is important to note that Luttrell's collection was broad. His collection of poetry was described by Edmond Malone, who saw it as it was being auctioned, as "twenty-four quarto volumes, distinguished by the letters of the alphabet." See Edmond Malone, *The Critical and Miscellaneous Prose Works of John Dryden* (London, 1800), 1:156.

9   Osborn, "Reflections on Narcissus Luttrell," 5.

10 Sharpe, *Reading Revolutions*, 277.

11 Sharpe, *Reading Revolutions*, 277.

12 Sharpe, *Reading Revolutions*, 279.

13 Osborn Shelves b 321, fol. 68.

14 Osborn Shelves b 321, fol. 68. In this respect, Luttrell's attitude resembles that of Sir William Drake: "a wary reader will not endeavor to remember the mass and whole bulk of books but only to extract the spirit and quintessence thereof and what is most applicable to business." See Sharpe, *Reading Revolutions*, 85.

15 Osborn Shelves b 321, fol. 106.

16 Osborn Shelves b 321, fol. 67.

17 Osborn Shelves b 321, fol. 64.

18 Jacques Bossuet, *A Pastoral Letter from the Lord Bishop of Meaux. To the New Catholicks of his Diocess, Exhorting them to keep their Easter* (1686), 3.

19 The commonplace books make his standing as a member of the National Church clear. Additionally, a receipt from the parish church of Chelsea dated 1714 notes that Luttrell obtained a pew "in the North Isle & ye South Side" of the church for his family. See Osborn Shelves c 65.

20 Osborn Shelves b 269, fol. 2.

21 The title page of *A Catechism Truly Representing the Doctrines and Practices of the Church of Rome* lists 1687 as its date of publication but Luttrell's record suggests that it was actually published in 1686.

22 Osborn Shelves b 321, fol. 160.

23 Osborn Shelves b 269, fol. 11.

24 Osborn Shelves b 321, fol. 67.

25 Osborn Shelves b 269, fol. 29.

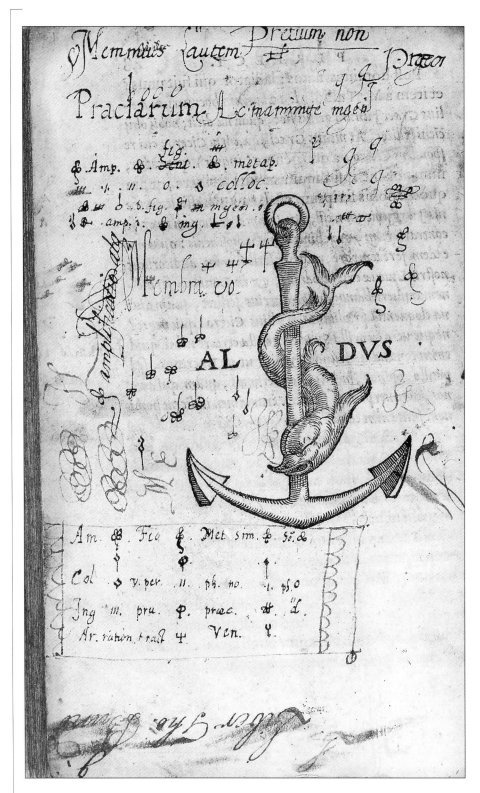

The last page of Marcus Tullius Cicero, *De oratore libri III*, Venice, 1569 (cat. no. 102).

"Rather soiled by use": Renaissance Readers and Modern Collectors

William H. Sherman

Here are two twentieth-century descriptions of sixteenth-century books:

". . . black letter, each title within a woodcut border; the blank margin . . . skilfully renewed; each work rather soiled by use but sound copies. . . ."

"This volume, printed during the reign of Elizabeth I, has been well and piously used. Marginal notations in an Elizabethan hand—comments and scriptural quotation—bring to life an early and earnest owner."

These two passages in fact describe the same volume. It is a small folio, now housed at the Huntington Library, containing the 1586 Book of Common Prayer and the 1583 Psalter.[1] It was among the unusual collection of more than 700 rare prayer books assembled by the businessman James R. Page and donated to the Huntington (of which he was a Trustee) just before his death in 1962. The first description of the volume is from the January 1952 catalogue of Bernard Quaritch Ltd., from whom Page acquired the book for the asking price of $210.[2] The second text is from the catalogue accompanying a 1953 exhibition at the Huntington, where Page's books were first displayed.[3] What the sale catalogue describes as "soil" is, as the exhibition catalogue makes clear, a thorough set of manuscript notes by a contemporary reader.

The phrasing in the Quaritch catalogue reflects a preference for clean texts that is so familiar to modern readers—even to those who are not familiar with the technical vocabulary of rare book catalogues—it may hardly seem worth pointing out. Most of us are told not to write in books at some point in our upbringing, and it is now one of the basic rules of what Paul Saenger and Michael Heinlen have described as "modern book etiquette, which views the printed page as sacrosanct and consequently all handwritten additions to the printed page as . . . detrimental to subsequent common use."[4] But the desire for pristine copies of books has a complex history that has yet to be written, with important implications for those who buy, preserve, and study the books that come down to us from the past.[5]

We might expect the preference for clean copies to be an article of professional faith among those who trade in rare books where, as in the trade of used goods of any kind, those that are in better condition tend to fetch a higher price. Not surprisingly, booksellers have used various methods to improve the condition of books by removing their 'flaws' (including, in some cases, the handwriting of earlier owners). The most aggressive practices, common in the eighteenth and nineteenth centuries and by no means unknown in the twentieth, involved bleaching the pages and cutting their margins down to the edge of the printed text.[6] Roger Stoddard has recently offered a vivid summary of these methods which, while perhaps unfair to today's more sensitive conservators, has chilling ramifications for the history of reading: "Rare is the binder who has deliberately preserved historical evidence. Old covers and endpapers are jettisoned along with their library marks, ownership marks, booksellers' marks, index notes, annotations, documents, or verses. . . . Then stains, both finger marks and marginalia, are bathed away in bleach before the results are squeezed flat in a standing press. . . ."[7] The treatment received by Page's prayer book was apparently more benign: the Quaritch catalogue indicates that the frayed margins of some of the leaves have been "skilfully renewed" by adding patches of blank paper. The language here suggests, however, an attempt to take the book back through time by undoing the signs of its subsequent use. The ideal copy becomes, paradoxically, a historic book with most of the traces of its history removed (even if, in this case, this was a matter of replacing what history itself had removed).

These practices have not been endorsed by all dealers, and the values behind them have not been shared by all collectors. For Page himself, readers' marks added to rather than detracted from the value of the book. As he put it in an interview with the *Los Angeles Times* during his 1953 exhibition, "Many of the books in my collection are enlivened by the marginal notes and comments made by the many people, from distinguished and well-known people to otherwise unknown persons, through whose hands they passed through the four centuries."[8] The rare book dealer Bernard M. Rosenthal, whose collection of annotated Renaissance books was recently acquired by the Beinecke Library at Yale, has explained that when he started buying books in the 1950s, "early printed books stained with the occasional fingerprints of a fifteenth-century pressman, or filled with scribblings by a contemporary student . . . did not have the same appeal to the bibliophiles as the flawless, virginal copy—even now one sometimes finds dealers' and auction catalogues in which the presence of manuscript annotations is mentioned in the same breath with the defects, e.g. 'some waterstains, occasional manuscript notes, else fine.'" A typical example can be found in another, much earlier, Quaritch catalogue where a book printed in Mexico in 1563 is described as "a perfect copy, large and fine, but having some MS. notes written in the sixteenth and seventeenth century. . . ."[9] A very recent Quaritch catalogue offers a poignant example of the kind of "restoration" such values could inspire. It describes a first edition of Milton's *Areopagitica* with two manuscript notes which are "very faint . . . all but washed out during some restoration in the past": comparison with other copies reveals that these notes were most likely corrections in the hand of Milton himself.[10] In this (hopefully) extreme case, the desire to take a book back to its original state—or our image of its original state—has obliterated the hand of the author who produced it, an act which is all the more ironic considering Milton's famous assertion in this very text that books "doe contain a potencie of life in them . . . as active as that soule was whose progeny they are; nay they do preserve as in a violl the purest efficacie and extraction of that living intellect that bred them."[11]

For Rosenthal, buying annotated books turned out to be a good way of competing with buyers who had more money. But it gradually produced a different view of what makes rare books valuable, and a different set of attitudes toward the scribbles of past readers. Rosenthal became "obsessed, by the idea of some day . . . producing a catalogue of books in which the presence of annotations would not merely be mentioned, but in which the manuscript portions would be ranked on the same level as the printed text and dignified by proper descriptions which would call attention to and emphasize their importance as primary sources for a great variety of topics. . . ." In 1997 Rosenthal published just such a catalogue of 242 annotated books, with wonderfully detailed descriptions of the length, content, and appearance of the marginalia.[12]

Henry Clay Folger was another twentieth-century collector with a special interest in annotated books. On 9 July 1931, a bookseller named N. M. Broadbent wrote to the newly appointed supervisor of research at the Folger Library, Dr. Joseph Quincy Adams, to describe some books he had sent to Folger containing annotations by sixteenth- and seventeenth-century readers. Broadbent suggested that "The subject of book annotations has, as far as I know, received no attention as yet from men of letters, but it is surely worthy of the deepest study." While "the late Sir Israel Gollancz was attracted to the subject" he did not have time to pursue it, and as "a branch of book collection" Broadbent believed it to be "peculiar to Mr. Folger—all other great collectors appearing to be unaware of the great importance of these books." Indeed, Broadbent reported Folger as saying "on one occasion that he [Folger] fully believed that when they came to be thoroughly examined many hitherto unknown facts and inferences would be supplied."[13]

Among the books Broadbent had sold to Folger, he wanted to draw Adams's attention to one of particular importance: a copy of Cicero's *De Oratore*, published by the Aldine press in 1569.[14] The extensive marginal annotations by a contemporary reader feature a complex code of symbols. While similar marks appear in other annotations from the period, this may be the first known case where the reader has provided a key to their meanings. On the last page of the volume, there are two versions of this key (see illustration pp. 84 and 145): there are some slight differences between them and some symbols in the text that do not appear in the key (suggesting that the method was still being worked out), but they do reveal a fairly elaborate system for tagging passages on particular topics (a trident was used for passages of argumentation or reasoning and the symbol for Venus signalled an interest in love) and employing particular rhetorical devices (such as 'amp[lificatio]', 'metap[hor]', and 'sim[ile]', each of which is signified by a symbol that looks like a flower). Picking up on the trefoil (or flower) symbol that had been found in some of Francis Bacon's notes, Broadbent claimed that this was the very system devised by Bacon and shared by Ben Jonson. In the letter to Adams he identified the key in the Cicero as being in Jonson's own hand, and Adams duly endorsed the letter, "Key to Annotated Books by Bacon and Jonson."

Folger assembled his collection, and cultivated his interest in annotated books during what Robert Alan Shaddy has recently called the Anglo-American "cult of collecting" of the late-nineteenth and early-twentieth centuries.[15] Shaddy suggests that one of the defining features of this movement was a fascination with books that had a documented connection to famous people from the past—what are called "association copies" in the trade. Raymond Blathwayte explained their attraction in a 1912 article on "The Romance of the Sale Room":

> As the years roll on the value of a book is often gauged by its associations, by its own individual history, by some special fact of interest connected with its owners, and, most especially of all, by any autographic value which those owners may have attached to it. There are books to-day which, by reason of pencilled margins or autographed presentations, possess a hundred times their original value or the value they would otherwise have possessed, and your true book collector is well aware of this.[16]

It is not hard to see how the signature and marginalia of Bacon or Jonson would be seen as a source of added value, and how an association with a famous writer could become a greater source of value than the physical condition of the book. William Harris Arnold, who created one of the period's most impressive libraries of association copies, suggested that the collector of early editions should strive "to procure them in their pristine state . . .; but, when a book bears evidence of a distinguished association, the material condition of the volume becomes a matter of secondary importance. . . . A volume of the very slightest consequence may be transformed into an object of precious regard just by a bit of writing on one of its leaves."[17] Or, at least in one extraordinary case, by a bit of soil on one of its leaves—Blathwayte told this story of a volume made more valuable after a royal reader dropped it in the road: "Charles I borrowed a volume of tracts from Thomason, the stationer, and clumsily let them fall into the mud, whereby their then value was considerably depreciated. Today the British Museum regards those stains as out-weighing by far the intrinsic value of the quaint old verbosities they so sadly dim."[18]

One of the standard guides to book collecting captures the current appeal of—and limits to—such association: "If the name is that of a well-known person, it adds to the value of the book, converting it into an 'association copy'. If the name is unknown, it is best that it should be unobtrusive, neat and not on the title-page."[19] Modern scholars are fortunate that not all collectors restricted their interest in a book's associations to the signatures and notes of famous people. An eloquent justification for collecting books with famous and not-so-famous associations—and one that anticipates the sentiments of Page and Rosenthal—can be found in the tribute paid by Charles Grosvenor Osgood to the library of A. Edward Newton (which was almost entirely devoted to association copies):

> Who in all the centuries have touched this book as I am touching now? Or how many generations has it passed, quiet and undisturbed, on a darkened shelf, enclosing its own dateless life, while the life of men swirled and eddied, around it unconcerned? . . . To the rightful owner the value of an old book is not a mere matter of date and scarcity. From all its previous owners and readers, *known or unknown*, has accrued to it a certain *potential of humanity* which is more than a mere matter of sentiment.[20]

If it was relatively easy to obliterate the signs of former owners, it was even easier to create associations with them after the fact, or invent them altogether. The most celebrated example of forced—or forged—associations involving a Renaissance author is the so-called Ireland Shakespeare Forgeries of the 1790s, in which William Henry Ireland faked signatures, letters, and even works by Shakespeare (see cat. no. 36).[21] But the methods for engineering associations need not be as devious as outright forgery, and an interesting association copy at the Huntington Library points to more ambiguous, and understandable, motives. On the title page of George of Montemayor's *Diana* (published in London in 1598) Ben Jonson clearly inscribed his signature ("*Sum Ben: Jonsonij*") and his motto ("*tanquam explorator*").[22] These notes are genuine, but their associations with this volume are not: the title page was detached from the copy Jonson originally owned and pasted into this one.

Broadbent's association of his annotated books with Jonson and Bacon needs to be put in the context not only of attitudes and practices within the booktrade but also of the Baconian movement in the early decades of the twentieth century. In arguing that Bacon wrote the plays attributed to Shakespeare, the Baconians found his signature everywhere (and, above all, encoded within the texts of Shakespeare's plays). In 1912 Broadbent's contemporary W. T. Smedley claimed to have worked with his fellow Baconian W. M. Safford to recover "nearly 2,000 books" annotated by Bacon.[23] Despite Folger's obvious allegiances to Shakespeare rather than Bacon, he acquired many of these volumes from Smedley. An article by G. R. Rose in the journal *Baconiana* (April 1945) offered a survey of what it claimed were the marks used in annotations by Bacon and Jonson, and mentioned that the books on which it was based "were collected by the late Mr. W. T. Smedley, and are now preserved in a famous American library."[24] At the time, this earned Folger the admiration of the book-collecting community: in 1932 *The Librarian and Book World* reported that his "most astounding achievement" as a collector "consisted in the re-formation of considerable portions of the libraries of Ben Jonson and Francis Bacon, including the acquisition of the famous collection *en bloc* of Messrs. W. T. Smedley and W. M. Safford."[25]

Sadly, there is no evidence whatsoever connecting the 1569 Cicero with Jonson or Bacon. In his discussion of Bacon in the *Index of English Literary Manuscripts*, Peter Beal concludes, "In so far as it relates to Bacon, Safford's collection was based on nothing more than fanciful conjecture. Many men besides Bacon were in the habit of marking their books, and also of using the marginal trefoil which is found in certain of Bacon's MSS. Without clear evidence of provenance or positive paleographical identification it would be impossible to distinguish Bacon's books from those of his contemporaries."[26] The marks found in Folger's 1569 Cicero are similar to those used by many readers, and the hand used to inscribe them does not bear any resemblance to that of either Jonson or Bacon. There is nothing to suggest that the volume had made its way to England until well after their deaths.

This episode provides a fascinating glimpse of Folger as collector. Like Page and Rosenthal's appreciation of annotated copies, and Arnold and Newton's passion for association copies, Folger's dealings with Broadbent and Smedley raise the larger question of what exactly gives old books their value in the present. The books and readers examined here point to two very different economies—two opposing philosophies—of collecting. Are annotated books 'soiled by use' or 'enlivened by association'? Are books from the past precious relics, in which marginalia are dirt or desecration, or are they inanimate objects which are only brought to life by traces of the human hands that used them? Folger was not the only modern collector who preferred his books dirty.[27]

1   The Book of Common Prayer is STC 16311.3 and the Psalter is STC 2463. The shelf-mark at the Huntington Library is RB 438000:87.

2   The text is now taped to a flyleaf at the front of the book. The details of the purchase are noted in Page's acquisitions records in the Huntington Library archives.

3   Dorothy Bowen, *The Book of Common Prayer: The James R. Page Collection* (Los Angeles, CA, 1953), 6.

4   Paul Saenger and Michael Heinlein, "Incunable Description and Its Implication for the Analysis of Fifteenth-Century Reading Habits," in *Printing the Written Word: The Social History of Books, circa 1450–1520*, Sandra L. Hindman, ed. (Ithaca, NY, 1991), 254.

5   Stephen Orgel has described this desire as "one of the strangest phenomena of modern bibliophilic and curatorial psychology." See "Margins of Truth," in *The Renaissance Text: Theory, Editing, Textuality*, Andrew Murphy, ed. (Manchester, 2000), 91–107 at 92.

6   Monique Hulvey, "Not So Marginal: Manuscript Annotations in the Folger Incunabula," *The Papers of the Bibliographical Society of America* 92 (1998): 159–76 at 161.

7   Roger Stoddard, "Looking at Marks in Books," *The Gazette of the Grolier Club*, n. s. 51 (2000): 27–47 at 32.

8   *Los Angeles Times* (June 7, 1953): IA:6. The clipping can now be found in the Huntington's institutional archives (folder 12.14.2.4).

9   Item 601 in *Monuments of Typography and Xylography . . . in the Possession of Bernard Quaritch and Offered for Sale at the Affixed Prices* (London, 1897).

10 Orgel, "Margins of Truth," 92.

11 John Milton, *Areopagitica* (London, 1644), sig. A3v.

12 Bernard M. Rosenthal, *The Rosenthal Collection of Printed Books With Manuscript Annotations: A catalog of 242 editions mostly before 1600 annotated by contemporary or near-contemporary readers* (New Haven, CT, 1997). The quotations in this paragraph can be found on p. 9.

13 Letter from Broadbent to Adams, 9 July 1931 (Folger Shakespeare Library, Archives, Correspondence Files, "Special Collections and Subjects," "Broadbent" folder), pp. 1–4 (cat. no. 106). An earlier letter from Broadbent to Folger himself (dated 2 May 1927), offering him his entire collection of annotated books for £7,500 is also in this folder.

14 Cat. no. 102.

15 Robert Alan Shaddy, "A World of Sentimental Attachments: The Cult of Collecting, 1890–1930," *The Book Collector* 43 (1994): 185–200.

16 Raymond Blathwayte, "The Romance of the Sale Room," *Fortnightly Review* (November 1912): 939–50 at 939.

17 William Harris Arnold, *Ventures in Book Collecting* (New York, 1923), 27–28.

18 Blathwayte, "The Romance of the Sale Room," 940.

19 G. L. Brook, *Books and Book-Collecting* (London, 1980), 88.

20 *Rare Books, Original Drawings, Autograph Letters and Manuscripts Collected by the Late A. Edward Newton*, 3 vols. (New York, 1941), unpaginated preliminaries to volume 1; my emphasis.

21 See, e.g., Bernard Grebanier, *The Great Shakespeare Forgeries* (New York, 1965).

22 Huntington Library, RB 62717.

23 William T. Smedley, *The Mystery of Francis Bacon* (London, 1912), 13, 156–60.

24 G. R. Rose, "The Libraries of Bacon and Ben Jonson: How They Marked Their Books," *Baconiana* 27, no. 107 (April, 1945): 57–59.

25 Immerito [anon.], "The Folger Library Shakespeare Collection," *The Librarian and Book World* 21 (1932): 262–63. Smedley had used the pseudonym 'Immerito' in an earlier article in *Baconiana*, and it is possible that he penned this tribute himself. (From Folger files, it appears that Henry C. Folger did not acquire the Safford collection en bloc from Smedley but that the Safford collection went to one or two other owners/dealers before it was sold at Sotheby's in 1941, at which time the Folger Library acquired a number of, but not all, the books.–Ed.)

26 Peter Beal, *Index of English Literary Manuscripts*, Vol. 1: 1450–1625, Part 1: Andrewes-Donne (London, 1980), 20.

27 I am grateful to Suellen Towers and Elaine Shiner from the Folger Shakespeare Library for bringing the Broadbent letter, the 1569 Cicero, and the *Baconiana* article to my attention, and to Alan Jutzi from the Huntington Library for his assistance with materials related to James R. Page. Peter Beal and Henry Woudhuysen also provided useful advice on books owned—and not owned—by Bacon and Jonson.

Catalogue of the Exhibition

'All the world's a text, and all the men and women merely readers.'[1]

Reading is fundamental to human interaction and communication. Through Gutenberg's innovations in printing technology, reading, once the preserve of a small educated elite, was opened up to a much more diverse audience. Renaissance readers were as varied as kings and tradesmen, saints and sinners, celebrities and nonentities. Like us, they read to learn and improve skills; to attain moral enrichment and for spiritual contemplation; and for the sheer joy and pleasure of reading.

Early modern readers reveal themselves to us through their books. Exquisite decoration and extensive annotation are evidence that these books were well-used and well-loved. Personal interactions between reader and book provide important insights into the lives, thoughts, and concerns of a time far removed from our own. But despite a distance of 500 years and more, the habits of Renaissance readers closely resemble those of readers today.

1   A similar paraphrase was originally used by Michael Mendle in his H-Net review
    of Kevin Sharpe, *Reading Revolutions: The Politics of Reading in Early Modern England*
    (New Haven and London, 1999).

I. Production of Reading Material

'Naked ink and paper': Manuscript and Printed Reading Material

From the late-fifteenth century, books were produced using Johann Gutenberg's innovations in printing technology. Although printed books were more affordable and more accessible, manuscript books did not disappear. There were certain niche markets that the printing press could not serve. Medieval scribes were eclipsed by the printing press, but demand for the services of scriveners, or professional copyists, to copy reading material and legal documents continued. For centuries, manuscript remained as vital as print.

1

Joannes Verulanus Sulpitius.
Scansiones Sulpitii.
Colop: Venice, Per Gulielmum de Fontaneto, 1516.
Sig. A1r
PA 2333 S8 1516 Cage

The clothing of this medieval scribe reveals that he, like most contemporary scribes, was a cleric. A window provides plenty of light for his well-stocked workshop, and to his left, a book on a copy stand is ready to be transcribed. His female visitor offers plants for his inspection, possibly ingredients for the inks he uses to illuminate and rubricate the texts he copies.

2

Unidentified French writing book.
Bound with, Martin Billingsley (1591–1622). *The Pens Excellencie or The Secretaries Delighte.*
London, Solde by Io. Sudbury and George Humble, [1618?].
Plate: Letter *V*
STC 3062

Copybooks, or writing manuals, designed to teach the most common scripts to budding professionals, originated in Renaissance Italy and served to popularize humanist script throughout Europe. This plate illustrating how to form the letter *V* is from an unidentified French copybook. Bound with this is the first copybook printed in England and the first writing manual by an English writing master.

3

J. H. *The Compleat Clerk, Containing the Best Forms of All Sorts of Presidents, for Conveyances and Assurances.* 4th edition. London, G. Sawbridge, T. Roycroft, and W. Rawlins, [1677].
Engraved title page
Wing H43

Scriveners, who primarily copied legal documents, would find this volume a useful guide. They also produced books, plays, and separates (descriptions of political events) to order for individuals and for booksellers. Here an English scrivener consults with his client. Another important activity of the profession, lending money at interest, vastly improved the fortunes of John Milton's father, a scrivener by profession.

2

3 DETAIL

4
Esther Inglis (1571–1624).
Self-portrait.
1599.
X.d. 533

5
Les CL psaumes de David escrites en diverses
sortes de lettres par Esther Anglois François.
A Lislebourg en Escosse, 1599.
Psalm 34, fol. 36
V.a. 93
The Gift of Lessing J. Rosenwald

Esther Inglis was a Huguenot refugee to
Scotland. Trained by her mother, a French
calligrapher, she produced manuscript books
for elite readers. In this stunning manuscript
of the Psalms, created for Prince Maurice of
Nassau in 1599, she employed sixteen different
styles of handwriting, and may have embroidered the cover as well. (See also the red velvet
binding decorated with silver thread embroi-
dery and seed pearls on *Argumenta Psalmorum*
Davidis, 1608, cat. no. 90.)

6
Joseph Moxon (1627–1691).
Mechanick Exercises, or, The Doctrine
of Handy-works. The second volume applied to
the art of printing.
London, Printed for Joseph Moxon, 1683.
Sig. G1r
Wing M3014

Joseph Moxon, hydrographer to Charles II
and a fellow of The Royal Society, trained in
Holland as an engraver, mapmaker, globe
maker, and printer. His *Mechanick Exercises*
provided detailed guidance for manual crafts,
including typefounding and printing.
Published in monthly installments, Moxon's
instructions were revolutionary because they
codified information and methods in use for
centuries but never before recorded system-
atically. His description of the hand press, its
equipment, and its operation remains among
the best accounts available in English.

7
Jost Amman (1539–1591). Woodcuts, from
Hartmann Schopper (b. 1542). . . . *Omnium*
Illiberalium Mechanicarum.
Colop: Frankfurt ad Moenum, Apud
Georgium Corvinum, 1568.
GT 5770 S4 Cage

These scenes by the Swiss artist Jost Amman
are from a "book of trades" intended to
supplement ancient encyclopedias. Amman's
stylized views of craftsmen include several
of men engaged in aspects of printed
book production.

A
A papermaker, or vat man, holds the wire
form over a vat of rag pulp. His assistant
carries away dried sheets. Visible in the background are the blades of a mill for grinding
rags into pulp and a screw press for extracting
water from the freshly made paper.

B
Using ink balls, a printer spreads ink on a type
form while the pressman prepares to remove a
just-printed sheet from the press. Compositors
work at their type cases in the background,
where large windows provide ample light.

C
An illuminator colors letters and illustrations.
He might also provide rubrication marks, or
marks to instruct the reader, in the printed text.

D
Toward the rear of the bookbinder's shop, a
worker is sewing the pages of a book together
at a sewing frame. In the foreground, a binder
uses a plough to trim the edges of the volume
he is binding. To the left of this figure, on the
floor, a press holds a newly-bound book to
flatten it. Tools for trimming and shaping
wooden boards of bindings and for embossing
designs in leather covers hang on the walls.

7-A

7-B

7-C

7-D

'Print would then surpass all that was ever writ': Coexistence of Manuscript and Print

Even with the advent of printing, manuscript continued to be the medium in which many literary genres (like lyric poetry) and politically volatile texts (like news) were read. The relationship between manuscript and print was symbiotic and coexistent. Texts and ideas passed from manuscript to print, and back again in the form of commonplace books and separates. Discarded manuscripts were sometimes used for endpapers, wrappers, and even bindings or binding supports for printed reading materials.

8
Thomas Scott (1580?–1626).
Vox populi. Or newes from Spayne.
[London], 1620.
Title page
STC 22100 copy 1

9
Thomas Scott. *The Second Part of Vox Populi.*
Goricom [i.e. London], Ashuerus Janss.
[i.e. N. Okes and J. Dawson], 1624.
Title page
STC 22103 copy 1

10
Thomas Scott. *Vox populi. Or news from Spain.*
In, Manuscript miscellany, ca. 1620.
V.a. 310
Unfoliated

Vox Populi, an anti-Catholic, anti-Spanish pamphlet, was printed in seven editions in 1620. Suppressed by the government, it continued to circulate in manuscript. *The Second Part of Vox Populi* was printed in four editions in 1624. Its title page presents a portrait of the controversial Spanish Ambassador to England, Don Diego Sarmiento de Acuña, conde de Gondomar, whose chair was specially equipped to accommodate his anal fistula. This is one of only two known complete versions of the title page.

11
Livy. *Quae manifesto extant, librorum decades.*
Paris, Vaenundantur ipsi Ascensio, 1530. Colop: 1531.
Title page
PA 6452 A2 1530 Cage

Beautifully illustrating the symbiosis between print and manuscript, this Latin edition of Livy's *Decades* carries the printing-press device of Jodocus Badius Ascensius (1462–1535), author, editor, printer, and publisher. Parts of medieval vellum manuscripts have been used to line the book's contemporary binding. The endleaves are from a professional sixteenth-century copy of a sermon about the Good Samaritan, and an early modern owner/reader, Matthew Rendoll, wrote himself into the story of the book by placing his manuscript monogram in a roundel of the title-page border and his signature below the image. Marginalia throughout the text further reinforce the relationship between manuscript and print.

12
A collection of proverbs, apothegms . . . .
Manuscript, ca. 1650.
Fol. 15
V.a. 263
Illustrated on page 58

This collection of reading notes, or commonplace book, recently identified as Sir William Drake's, is one of about fifty surviving volumes of his notes. Drake read primarily political theory, like Machiavelli, and works influenced by it such as Ben Jonson's *Sejanus*. While Drake's personal political opinions were clearly

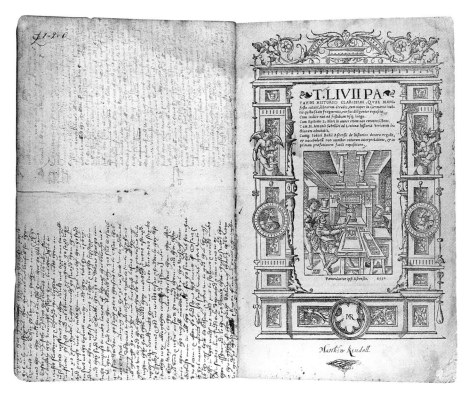

11

shaped by his reading, as a member of Parliament in the early 1640s and in the 1660s he was not a political activist.

13
Cardanus Rider. *Riders (1680) British Merlin.*
London, Tho. Newcomb, for the Company of Stationers, 1680.
Title page
Wing A2254.5

Riders British Merlin was a fixture in the "golden age" of English almanac publication between 1640 and 1700. Sarah Sales, a farmer and business woman, used this copy to record information about crops, laborers' wages, sales of produce, and debts owed her by family and others. Most almanacs were sold unbound. Owners frequently had them interleaved with blank pages for notes and fitted with metal clasps (now lost from this copy) to close the covers.

14
François Guyot, typefounder (?).
Type specimen sheet, ca. 1565.
STC 7758.3 vol. 3 no. 6

Six samples of roman type in various sizes, featuring upper and lower cases, extra vowels, dipthongs and syllables, punctuation, diacritics for foreign languages, and numerals are printed on this advertisement. The manuscript annotations in a mid- to late-sixteenth-century hand quote prices for the type, ranging from £4.13.3 for the largest to 22 "gylders" each for the two smallest. Prices given in guilders probably indicate this type was manufactured in the Low Countries, quite possibly by the Flemish typefounder François Guyot around 1565, before he emigrated to London. This specimen sheet is unique to the Folger collection.

'Blood . . . commands me use none other ink but red': Textual Guides for the Reader

Red is the color of blood, the original ink. It attracts attention and inspires action. Red ink in medieval manuscripts instructed readers how to interpret the text. The earliest printed books incorporated this manuscript tradition, using red ink either printed or applied by hand, and type that imitated handwriting. Black letter could be most easily read by the least literate readers. Consequently, it was used in a majority of accessible, widely-disseminated texts: hornbooks, service books, the Bible, royal proclamations, and statutes. Black letter and red ink represented authority on paper.

15

Great Britain. Laws, statutes, etc.
"A collection of statutes of the realm,
c. 1225–c. 1309."
Compiled ca. 1325.
Fols. 85v–86r
V.a. 256

An Anglo-Norman translation of the 1225 reissue of Magna Carta is included in this manuscript collection of statutes. Like medieval religious texts, the statutes are inscribed with decorated capitals and red and blue rubrication, indicating to the reader where new texts or passages begin. Other important information, such as fines and sums of money, are rubricated as well. The book's small format makes it portable, probably for the use of a justice of the peace or a circuit-riding judge.

16

Bible. New Testament. Coverdale.
The Newe Testament faythfully translated and latly corrected by Myles Coverdale.
[Antwerp, G. Montanus, 1538].
Sig. ✠viir
STC 2840

Miles Coverdale's New Testament, one of the first English translations, was printed in black letter. Red ink was used to signpost the text, a practice predating the numbering of verses in William Whittingham's 1560 translation, the Geneva Bible. Red ink was applied to textual features such as running heads, marginal lines, initial capitals, and other symbols, including manicules, or pointing hands.

17

Catholic Church. Primer.
Hereafter foloweth the prymer in Englysshe and in Latin.
Rouen, In edibus Roberti Valentini, 1555.
Sigs. B4v–B5r: December
STC 16071

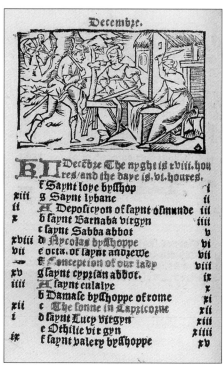

17

A simplified form of the Roman Catholic order of service, the Primer was intended for private devotions. The Kalendar, set in black letter, emphasized with red ink major holy days such as the "Nativity of Our Lord" on December 25, revealing the origin of 'red-letter days.' The Primer was the first service book produced cheaply and made widely available through printing. Consequently, it became a central text in childhood education.

18

Catholic Church. Manual.
Manuale ad usum per celebris ecclesie Sarisburiensis.
London, noviter impressum, 1554.
Fols. lxixv–lxxr
STC 16153

The Manual, containing ceremonies celebrated only occasionally, such as baptisms, weddings, and funerals, was a service book for priests. Its many instructions were printed in red ink. This edition dates from the reign of Mary I, who attempted to undo the Protestant Reformation of her father Henry VIII and her brother Edward VI. Mary's *Manuale* was backward-looking in all its forms, returning to the traditional Salisbury usage in Latin, printed in black letter. It was also the last version to include music.

19

Francis Bacon, viscount St. Albans (1561–1626).
De sapientia veterum, liber.
London, Excudebat Felix Kyngston, impensis Iocosae Norton & Richardi Whitaker, 1634.
Sigs. B4v–B5r
STC 1129

Informal, secular use of red ink also served to instruct and guide readers. In this Latin edition of *The Wisdom of the Ancients*, a reader used red ink, long a delineator of textual boundaries, to construct a margin-within-a-margin. Inside these limits, the reader transliterated the text or made notes in shorthand,

which was just becoming popular in the 1630s. The red ink of ancient usage authorized the novelty of shorthand in a printed text.

20

Samuel Daniel (1562–1619).
The Collection of the Historie of England.
London, Printed for Simon Waterson, 1626.
Sigs. G3v–G4r
STC 6251 copy 4

A reader of this authorized version of early English history has annotated the printed text in red ink. Like liturgical rubrication, his red ink marks instruct readers where and what to read. The markings include underlining (especially of the names of monarchs) as well as symbols drawn in the margins.

21

Clement Walker (1595–1651).
Anarchia anglicana: or, The history of Independency. The second part.
[London?], Printed in the year 1649.
Sig. O4r
Wing W317 bound with W334

For many in the mid-seventeenth century, the supreme horror of the English civil wars was the execution of Charles I. A list of the regicides who signed the king's death warrant was printed in red ink in this contemporary history. Red ink invoked its ancient origins in blood—this time royal blood—and authorized the bloody indictments imposed on the regicides after the Restoration.

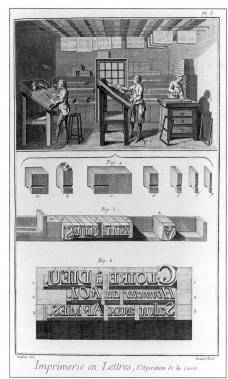

Imprimerie en Lettres, L'Operation de la Casse

22-I

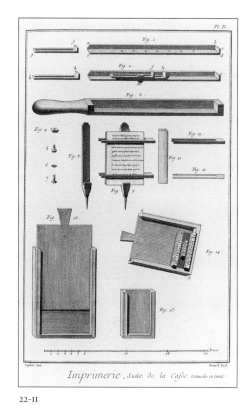

Imprimerie, Suite de la Casse, ustensiles et outils.

22-II

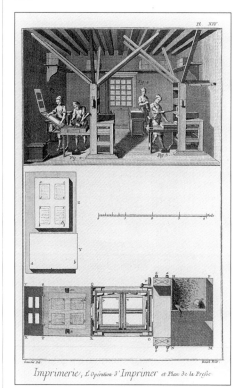

Imprimerie, L'Opération d'Imprimer et Plan de la Presse.

22-XIV

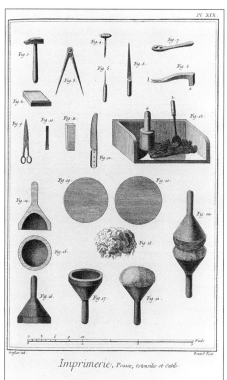

Imprimerie, Presse, ustensiles et outils.

22-XIX

22
Louis-Jacques Goussier.
Imprimerie (Plates I, II, XIV, XIX).
Engravings by Robert Bénard, from
*Encyclopédie ou Dictionnaire raisonné des
sciences, des arts, et des métiers . . . Recueil
de planches.*
Paris, Briasson, 1762–72.
AE 25 E5 Cage

Plates I and II show compositors, or typesetters,
and their tools. The letters and punctuation
marks most frequently needed were placed
within easy reach in the lower part of the type
case. Those used less frequently, such as capitals, were placed in the top of the case. Thus
the distinction of 'upper' and 'lower' case
letters originated.

Using a composing stick, the compositor
arranged the letters of each word, sentence,
and page in a mirror image of the eventual
printed page. When the stick was full, the type
was transferred to a galley, or tray, from which
proof impressions were then made. The spac-
ing elements highlighted here were important
in determining the ultimate format of a page
of type. In the earliest days of the hand press,
a compositor might set three pages of forty-
two lines each in a ten-hour work day.

Plates XIV and XIX depict a hand press, or
common press, and the tools necessary to
operate it. The hand press remained essentially
the same as the one developed by Gutenberg
until the eighteenth century. Prominent
among the small hand tools are the ink balls
used to spread ink on the forms of set type.
Ink balls were stuffed with wool or horse hair
and covered with carefully prepared grease-
free leather, to which the printing ink would
adhere. A pressman, or beater, held one ink
ball in each hand, distributing the ink evenly
over the type with circular motions. An experienced team could produce, on average, two
hundred impressions in an hour.

23
Jan van der Straet (1523–1605). Printing shop.
Engraving by Théodore Galle, from *Noua
Reperta.*
Antwerp, ca. 1600.
Art vol. f81 no. 4

Jan van der Straet's *Noua Reperta* celebrates
Renaissance technologies and discoveries. In
this engraving of a printing shop, compositors
stand at type cases topped by manuscript texts
in visoriums. A proofreader, wearing spectacles, and a corrector are also at work. Tables
are stacked with dry, printed sheets of books
in production. There are two printing presses,
one for proof and one for printing the final
text. An ink pot rests on a table next to a
pressman who inks a type form with ink balls.
Between the two presses freshly printed sheets
dry on a line. The master printer pulls the bar
to impress a sheet of paper on the inked type
form as he chats with a scholar or author.

II. Consumption of Reading Material

'From the most able, to him that can but spell': Learning to Read

English children were taught to read by their mothers or petty schoolmasters from hornbooks or other basic reading manuals printed in black letter. They advanced from the ABC to the Primer. Female education often stopped at this level. Some readers could read printed black letter but not handwritten italic scripts, and many, especially women, had only limited ability to write. An inability to write even one's own name, however, did not necessarily indicate an inability to read.

24

[*The A. B. C. with the Lord's Prayer*].
[London?, 1625].
Hornbook
STC 13813.6

Hornbooks were originally constructed of a sheet of paper, containing the alphabet, vowels, syllables, and the Lord's Prayer printed in black letter, nailed to a piece of wood and covered with a sheet of horn. The wood on the verso of this hornbook has been overlaid with leather embossed with an image of St. George. From this simple and practical device, most early modern English children learned reading and fundamental lessons in obedience, respect for authority, and good citizenship.

24

25

John Hart (d. 1574).
A methode or comfortable beginning for all unlearned, whereby they may be taught to read English.
London, Henrie Denham, 1570.
Sigs. B1v–B2r
STC 12889

John Hart campaigned for spelling reform in late-sixteenth-century England, arguing that historical misunderstanding of letters and sounds made reading unduly difficult. Taking his lead from similar Continental movements, he modified Anglo-Saxon, Latin, Greek, and other letters into an easy-to-write phonetic alphabet of twenty-five symbols. Hart eliminated *c*, *q*, *y*, and *w* but adopted *j* and provided additional symbols, such as the Saxon *thorn* for *th*. Hart was convinced that anyone could learn to read quickly and easily using his alphabet. Here, in the only known complete copy of this work, pictorial examples provide pronunciation for each symbol.

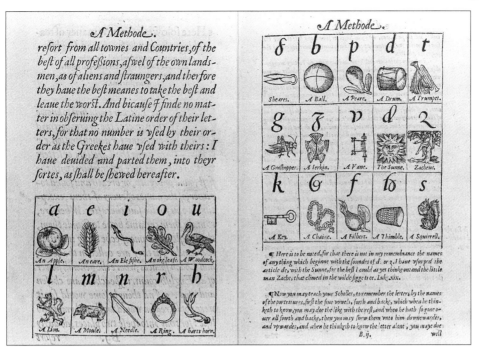

25

26

S. W. A.

Most easie instructions for reading, specially penned for the good of those who are come to yeares.

[London, ca. 1610].

Pp. 2–3 (unsigned)

STC 17

This manual for teaching adults to read has instructions for the teacher printed in roman type and the text for the student printed in black letter. Its format is markedly different than the hornbooks for children, and its content is more sophisticated. Included with the alphabet are examples of vowels, dipthongs, abbreviations, "the variable sound of some letters," "letters which in re-spect of their neare likenesse in com-bi-na-ti-on, are hardly known," and passages from the Psalms.

27

Church of England.

Catechismus paruus pueris Primium latinae qui ediscatur, propendius in scholis. Translated by Alexander Nowell.

London, Apud Johannem Dayum, 1573.

Title page

STC 18711

The "shorter catechism" consisted of the seven penitential psalms and other devotional material from the Church of England's *Book of Common Prayer*. The title-page illustration emphasizes learning through reading. Boys diligently read under the eye of their instructor, while one is about to receive a reward either for reciting or responding to questions. This Latin translation was intended for students beginning Latin study, an advanced level of education. At this level students were required to learn to read roman type. This is the only known copy of the first edition.

GRAMMATICA

29

28
Francis Quarles (1592–1644).
Emblems.
London, Printed for J: W: and F: E:, 1663.
Sig. V8r
Wing Q80

Early modern educational theorists considered
reading and writing separate processes and
taught them as such. Ordinary readers
and writers, however, connected the two, as
did Grace Feary, who found space to practice
writing her ABCs in one of the bestselling
seventeenth-century English emblem books.
Margins and other blank spaces in early printed
books were viewed as areas intended for
writing. Printed letters provided convenient
models to imitate, and the content of the text
inspired thoughts to be jotted down.

29
Franz Cleyn (1582–1658).
Grammatica. From, *Septem liberales Artes.*
[London], Sold by Tho. Hinde, 1645.
Plate 7
Acc. 226267

Grammar, one of the seven liberal arts, is
portrayed as a mother teaching the children
at her skirts to read and write. A boy receives
instruction in writing his ABCs. A girl standing
to the side reads from a book. She is literally
and figuratively excluded from the knowledge
of writing, reinforcing the traditional notion
that males should be taught to read AND
write, but females only to read.

'Give me that glass, and therein I will read': The Technology of Reading

Reading in Renaissance Europe was expanded and enhanced through numerous technological innovations, among them mechanized book stands, or book wheels, spectacles, and magnifying lenses. Spectacles pre-dated Gutenberg, but the proliferation of printed books increased the desire and need to read and promoted their use. Intensified reading also provoked a need for new and improved light sources.

30
Jan van der Straet (1523–1605).
Spectacle maker.
Engraving by Jan Collaert, from *Noua Reperta*.
Antwerp, ca. 1600.
Art vol. f81 no. 15

The shop of this spectacle maker is conveniently located in the market, across from the scrivener's stall. Most of the figures in the scene are using spectacles to read. Glass lenses to improve vision were developed by Islamic scientists in the eleventh century. Venice, a center of glassmaking, was manufacturing spectacles by the opening of the fourteenth century, and a spectacle-maker's guild was formed there in 1320. A fairly widespread use of spectacles predated the mass production of reading material with the printing press, and it has been suggested that improved readers' vision stimulated the demand for more reading material rather than more reading material stimulating the need for spectacles.

Iean. Stradanus inuent.   Ioän. Collaert sculp.   Ban. Galle incid.
CONSPICILLA.
Inuenta conspicilla sunt, quæ luminum   Obscuriores detegunt caligines.

30

31
The myrrour [and] dyscrypcyon of the worlde with many meruaylles.
[London, 1527?] Colop: Enprynted by me Laurence Andrewe.
Sig. hivr
STC 24764

Tools available to early modern readers and writers included revolving book stands with internal storage space, inkwells, and penners (pen cases). All are visible in an image probably intended to represent the author. He wears a pained expression, and the floor of his study is strewn with sheets of paper or vellum covered in writing. His motivation for creating this book, expressed in the prologue as a need to preserve knowledge of the seven liberal arts and other fundamental skills, made the volume itself a technological tool for readers.

32
William Shakespeare (1564–1616).
Mr. William Shakespeare's comedies, histories, and tragedies.
London, By Isaac Iaggard and Ed. Blount, 1623.
Sig. Bb6v
STC 22273 no. 46

An early reader tucked in a pair of spectacles at the end of act 5, scene 1, of *The Winter's Tale* and apparently forgot about them. Their rusty outline is clearly visible in an otherwise clean copy of the First Folio, providing the only indication this book was ever read.

33

33
[John White (d. 1671)].
A rich cabinet with variety of inventions . . .
Collected by J. W., a lover of artificial conclusions.
4th edition, with many additions.
London, Printed for William Whitwood, 1668.
Sig. B1v
Wing W1791

"How to make a glorious light with a Candle, like the Sun-shine" is illustrated in John White's collection of helpful hints. A blown glass globe "bigger than a penny loaf" was to be filled with the purest water available. Ideally it would be suspended from a stick placed in "a hole in a post in the wall." A lighted candle set behind the globe shines through the water to provide a bright, safe light for reading or other close work.

34
Gregorio Leti (1630–1701).
Critique historique, politique, morale, economique & comique, sur les lotteries . . .
Traduit de l'Italien . . .
[par Pierre Ricotier]. Vol. 1.
Amsterdam, Chez Theodore Boeteman, 1697.
Engraved title page
Acc. 226891

"Criticism," personified as a female reader, graces a book exposing the excesses of lotteries. The author attempts to rehabilitate the criticism genre by distancing it from exaggeration and hyperbole. The figure surrounded by measuring instruments conveys precision and moderation. This image depicts the thorough reader envisioned by the author—bespectacled, holding a square in her left hand and a dividing compass in her right. A ruler, a protractor, a quadrant, and a level lie nearby. On the wall behind her, a candle in front of a mirror increases the amount and quality of available light.

34

35
Spectacles.
Seventeenth century.
Generously lent by the Pilgrim Society,
Pilgrim Hall Museum, Plymouth, MA

Leather-covered horn frames, with a high
curved nosepiece and no ear temples, was
a style of spectacles familiar in Europe from
the fifteenth century. Horn was flexible
enough to hold spectacles on the nose
(although this placement sometimes interfered
with breathing) prior to the development of
temples in England in the 1730s. Correction was
based on age rather than actual deterioration of
eyesight, and these glass lenses provided only
slight magnification. This pair of spectacles is
believed to have belonged to Peter Brown,
who arrived at Plymouth aboard *The
Mayflower* in 1620.

36
*Imitatio Christi. Liber de imitatione Christi
cum tractatu de Cordis meditatione.*
[Cologne, 1503].
Binding incorporating a case for spectacles
Generously lent by Catholic University of
America Library

Printed in Cologne in 1503 by a printer identified only through the location of his shop
(*Retro Minores*),[1] these two works were often
printed together in fifteenth- and sixteenth-
century editions. The second work usually
began on the final page of the *Imitatio Christi*,
as though the two were one continuous text.
This copy is bound in blind-tooled leather
over wooden boards lined with waste vellum
manuscripts, and an owner hollowed out a
convenient storage space for spectacles.
Devotional works in small formats might well
have been carried in pocket or pouch so the

owner could read at convenient times. Having spectacles handy would have facilitated such occasional reading, and spectacles might have been necessary to read the small print. In March 1455, Aeneas Silvius Piccolomini (later Pope Pius II) wrote from Frankfurt am Main to Cardinal Juan de Carvajal about Gutenberg's just-printed Bible: "'I did see various parts of the text, in very fine and proper letters which your Honour could read without any trouble and without using your glasses.'"[2] Additional aids for readers of this volume were vellum turkshead knots to indicate sectional divisions in the text. Among later owners who have left their marks in this book is the Reverend Arthur T. Connolly who donated it to the Catholic University of America, Washington, DC.

Barbara Henry
Marilyn Barth
Catholic University of America Library

1 *Retro Minores*," behind the Minors, suggests that the printing shop was located behind the cloister of the Franciscans, also known as the Friars Minor.

2 Quoted in John Dreyfus, "The Invention of Spectacles and the Advent of Printing," *The Library*, 6th ser., 10 (1988): 93–106, at 102.

37
George James De Wilde, attributed to.
The Seven Ages of Man (*As You Like It* 2.7).
Oil on canvas, 1823?
FPa 19 (Case no. 1831)

"To write and read comes by nature," Shakespeare wrote in *Much Ado About Nothing* (3.3.14). This painting represents another of Shakespeare's axioms, the seven ages of man, or the natural human life cycle. In the foreground, an ape engages in acts that come naturally to humans—reading and writing. A familiar trope from medieval and Renaissance painting, the 'literary ape' was often portrayed as a reader or an author. Surrounded by a collection of Ben Jonson's works and an eighteenth-century Shakespeare forgery, the ape holds a quill pen and writes in a First Folio edition of Shakespeare.

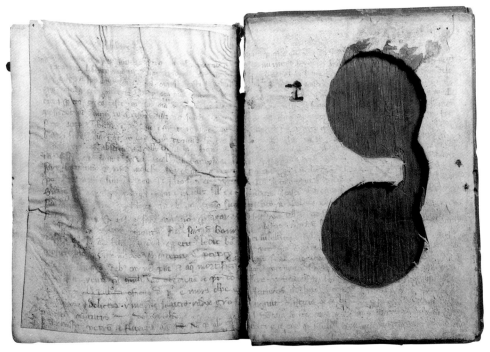

36

'Judge your six-pen'orth, your shillings worth, your five shillings worth':
Economies of Reading

Although mass production made printed books more affordable than those produced by hand, they were not cheap. In mid-seventeenth-century England, chapbooks sold for two pence, sermons for six pence, heavily illustrated works for £5 for a single volume (new), and multi-volume sets of antiquarian interest for £7 (used), putting them out of the reach of most people. Less affluent readers borrowed books, bought books in partnership, bought cheap, small editions, and supported a vigorous used-book business. Lavish editions were a rarity due both to cost of production and cost to consumers.

38
Wenceslaus Hollar (1607–1677).
Byrsa Londinensis, vulgo The Royall Exchange of London.
Etching, 1644.
Art vol. d86 no. 1

The Royal Exchange was a purpose-built commercial complex, primarily an emporium for high-end goods and services. It was also adjacent to one of the major concentrations of booksellers' shops in London. A few Stationers and printsellers had shops in the Exchange itself. Thomas Jenner, who sold the print of William of Orange (see cat. no. 59), was located there.

Hollar's etching accurately conveys the operation of the Exchange on two levels, literally as a structure, and figuratively as a cultural marketplace. The Exchange was where one went to purchase goods, and it was where one went for social exchange. Shops were located on the upper levels, in the Pawn and Upper Pawn, while the lower level courtyard and colonnade served as a common gathering place. Commercial transactions in the book and print shops were one mode of exchange of information and ideas. Gossip and the exchange of news in the courtyard was another. The sole female figure in the sea of humanity depicted by Hollar is a mercury woman, a news hawker, with her basket full of news and ballads.

39
Richard Tottel (d. 1593), ed.
Songes and sonets written by the right honorable Lord Henry Haward, late Earl of Surrey, and others.
[London], Apud Richardum Tottell, 1574.
Sigs. Cviv–Cviir
STC 13866 copy 1

Written primarily by Sir Thomas Wyatt, the elder, and his disciple, Henry Howard, earl of Surrey, this verse collection was an early bestseller. In the summer of 1557, the first three impressions sold out within fifty-six days. By 1587, five more editions had been printed. Designed for popular appeal, the miscellany introduced the poetic forms of the sonnet and free verse to a wide and enduring readership. The text was in black letter with italic for emphasis. An influential address to the reader exhorted "the unlearned, by readinge to learne to bee more skil full."

A Support For the Sinking Heart
19 Ser. Simon Ash
Gen 22. 14. Jehovah Jireth

Memmorandom
July ye 20.th 1747 This Book
was Joyntly Purchased by
Phillis Burton of Tisbury Wilts.
and Jane Scammell. of West
Hatch in Tisbury. Each to have
its use 6 Months of the year
and the Last life to claime
a Singular Rite to which we
Both Set our hands P. Burton
Jane Scammell

41

40
Gijsbert Voet (1589–1676).
Catalogus variorum librorum instuetissimae bibliothecae praestantissimi doctissimique.
London, Novembris 25, 1678. This catalogue is to be distributed gratis by M. Pitt, W. Nott, P. Parker, W. Leake, E. Millington, J. Hall, and J. Hooke.
Manuscript notes facing sig. G2v
Wing V675

Book auctions were a common occurrence by the late seventeenth century. Symbols, printed text, and red ink in this compendium catalogue of several large auctions provide a key to the source of the listed titles. Purchase price is indicated in the red-ruled margins. The entry for Sir William Dugdale's massive three-volume antiquarian study of English monastic lands, *Monasticon Anglicanum*, for example, shows it was purchased at Worstley's auction for £7 while another copy brought £7.4.0 at Pitt and Cooper's auction. (See illustration on page 66.)

41
Simeon Ashe (d. 1662).
A Support for the Sinking Heart in Times of Distresse.
London, By G. M. and are to be sold by Thomas Underhill, 1642 (and other titles).
Fol. 3 of manuscript notes at end of volume
Acc. 146894

In the early eighteenth century, dissenting Protestants Phyllis Burton and Jane Scammell jointly collected civil-war era sermons about religious sectarianism. Their signed "Memmorandum" stipulates that each had "use" of the resulting volume six months out of the year. The longest lived would have "Singular Rite" to it. Other manuscript notes include a finding guide for individual sermons in the assembled volume; a short history of Star Chamber, High Commission, and the Westminster Assembly of Divines; biographies of authors of the sermons; and a description of dissenter persecution.

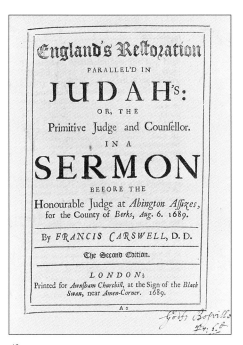

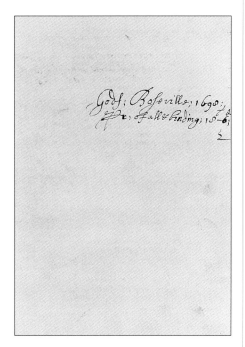

42

42
Francis Carswell (d. 1709).
Englands Restoration parallel'd in Judah's . . .
2d edition.
London, For Awnsham Churchill, 1689
(and other titles).
Sig. A2 of Carswell
Wing C650 copy 2 bound with S3348 copy 2

Godfrey Boseville accumulated sermons
delivered during the Glorious Revolution of
1688–89. He purchased them individually, had
them bound, then titled and indexed them as
a single volume. On the title page of each
sermon Boseville recorded the purchase price,
usually six pence, along with his signature and
place of purchase, other than London. On the
front flyleaf he notes the price of purchasing
and binding the entire collection: 18s. 6d.
(eighteen shillings, six pence). The volume
contains a single annotation correcting
grammar, which shows that Boseville read
with his pen nearby, albeit seldom used.

43
The Way to Heaven made playn.
London, By P. L. for W. Thackery, 1674
(one of eight chapbooks, 1672–1674,
bound together).
Title page with woodcut
Acc. 209224

Chapbooks were inexpensive moralistic texts,
aimed at instilling piety in the population at
large. The name derives from the petty chap-
men, or retailers, who sold them. Chapbooks
featured woodcut illustrations for visual
appeal and a text generally set in black letter,
designed to make them accessible to most
levels of literacy. Two contemporary male
owner/readers of this volume had the ability
both to read and to write. Of the eight chapbooks here, five are otherwise unknown.

44
Virgil.
Works of Publius Virgilius Maro.
Translated by John Ogilby.
London, Thomas Warren for the Author, 1654.
Tip-in between sigs. A1 and A2
Acc. 225452

In a later phase of his varied career, John
Ogilby was a pioneer publisher of fine illustrated volumes financed by pre-paid subscriptions. His translation of Virgil was printed in
"royal folio" using specially-designed initials
and headpieces, high-quality ink, and French
paper. This copy carries the hand-colored coat
of arms of Thomas Wriothesley, fourth earl of
Southampton. The 110 plates were designed by
the painter Francis Cleyn and engraved or
etched by the foremost practitioners of the
day—notably Wenceslaus Hollar, William
Faithorne, and Pierre Lombart. This edition
sold unbound for £5.

45

45
James I silver sixpence.
Elizabethan silver hammered shilling.
Elizabethan silver hammered sixpence.

46
Peter W. M. Blayney.
Colored and labeled site plan of Saint Paul's
Cathedral and surrounding buildings.
1991.
Map 234325
The Gift of Peter W. M. Blayney

There are no existing seventeenth-century
maps that sufficiently illustrate St. Paul's
Cathedral precincts, center of the early modern English book trade. Superimposed upon a
modern map of the Cathedral, and a limited
area around it, is an original site plan by Peter
W. M. Blayney reconstructing its configuration
circa 1623 (the year the Shakespeare First Folio
was published). Basing his work on contemporary leases and surveys made in the wake of
the 1666 Great Fire of London, Blayney reconstructed the locations of Stationers' shops
around the Cathedral, in particular those in
Paul's Cross Churchyard in the upper right of
this map.

Areas colored green on the map are gardens.
Grey delineates the Cathedral and its depen-
dencies, such as the bishop of London's palace
in the upper left of the Cathedral yard. Red
signifies other buildings in the precincts, many
of them related to the book trade. Identifiable
Stationers' shops are shown in yellow with the
name of the shop provided.

Blayney also constructed a model of one
of the largest book shops in Paul's Cross
Churchyard, known as the Three Pigeons
between 1614 and 1684 (see cat. no. 61).

‘Read here a little, that thou mayst know much’: Occasions of Reading

Reading served many purposes in early modern Europe. Students and scholars read to acquire specialized knowledge. Professionals read to enhance their skills. The accused read in pursuit of justice, the godly in search of salvation. Consumers read about new products. For women, studying worthy books might attract or repel suitors. Reading was often a pragmatic act, 'studied for action' to navigate the difficult course of human experience.

47

47
Jan Luyken (1649–1712).
Engraved title page, from William Sewel
(1653–1720). *A new dictionary . . . English
and Dutch.*
Amsterdam, By de Weduwe van Steven
Swart, 1691.
Engraved title page
Wing S2825

Renaissance dictionaries were products of
dawning nationalism. This dictionary was
designed to facilitate the Anglo-Dutch nationalism required by the accession of a Dutch
prince to the English throne as King William
III in 1689. On the title page, Jan Luyken, the
great Dutch poet-engraver, depicted readers
in a study or library consulting numerous
volumes. The scene suggests that reading,
especially informed scholarly reading, provides
a mechanism for overcoming not only linguistic
differences, but also cultural and political
ones. Communication skills learned through
reading would be vital to the success of the
new regime.

48
Thomas Littleton (1402–1481).
Littleton's Tenvres in English.
Colop: London, by Rycharde Tottill, 1586.
Sig. Kii
STC 15773

Sir Thomas Littleton's explication of the
complicated English system of landholding,
or land tenures, was essential reading for
early modern lawyers and law students. This
pocket-sized copy is interleaved with blank
pages intended for readers' notes. Annotations
in it are in black and red ink, in English and
Law French (the arcane language of English
law), and also include underlining in the text
and pointing hands in the margins.

49
Euclid.
*Preclarissimus liber elementorum
Euclidis perspicacissimi.*
Erhardus Ratdolt Augustensis impressor
solertissimum Venetijs impressit, 1482.
Sigs. b6v–b7r
INC E86

This rare first printed edition of Euclid's
Elements is illustrated with over 410 woodcut
and lead-line diagrams. Erhard Ratdolt,
the printer, made books beautiful to assist
students in reading difficult subjects. In black
letter with ornamental page borders, this
copy has uniquely decorated capitals, hand-
colored in alternating red and blue with
a yellow background. The book's beauty did
not deter early modern students of geometry
from proving theorems and making notes in
the margins.

50
Jacob Cats (1577–1660).
Spiegel van den ouden ande nieuwen tijdt.
The Hague, By Isaac Burchoorn, 1632.
Emblem xxv, sig. K2r
PN 6349 C2 S7 1632 Cage copy 2

In this love emblem, a woman uses reading to
avoid the attention of a suitor. Illustrating the
traditional proverb "birds of a feather flock
together," this scene is filled with pairs of birds
that mate for life. The poet warns humans
seeking similar mates that worldly men are
not ideally suited to women who would rather
read than engage in mating rituals. Cats also
implies that not all humans are suited to
reading and contemplation.

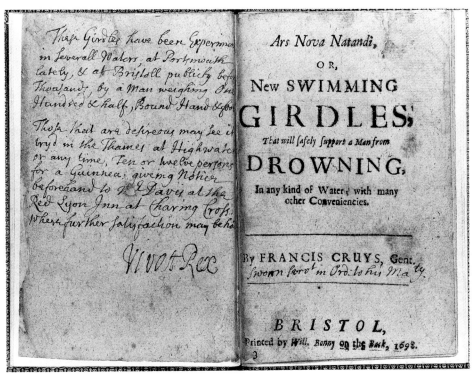

51

51
Francis Cruys (fl. 1697).
Ars nova natandi, or new swimming girdles.
Bristol, By Will. Bonny, 1693.
Manuscript notes facing title page
Wing C7447.5

Aristotle had only disdain for humans who
"could neither Swim, nor Read." He probably
would have approved of Cruys's invention to
aid swimmers and of the inventor's printed
publicity. The only known copy of this publication includes manuscript testimony about
the efficacy of swimming girdles (a type of
life jacket). It also informs the reader where
demonstations might be seen and girdles
might be purchased.

52
John Lilburne (1614?–1657), defendant.
*The triall of Lieut. Collonell John Lilburne . . .
London, the 24, 25, 26. of Octob. 1649.*
[London], By Hen. Hils, [1649].
Frontispiece
Wing W338

On trial for treason in October 1649, John
Lilburne was refused legal counsel by the
Cromwellian government. Forced to defend
himself, Lilburne prepared by reading essential
legal texts. To counter the charges against him,
he carried a number of law books to the bar
and read aloud from them. His trump card
turned out to be Sir Edward Coke's *Institutes*,
which he holds in his hand. To the amazement
of everyone, Lilburne won his case and
was acquitted.

The names of the Iury.
of life and death.

Stationers' shops were more than just places to purchase books. They carried a variety of items geared to the needs of readers and writers, for example, paper, styli, pen knives, quills, ink, and sealing wax. Certain shops specialized in maps and prints, and even globes and mathematical instruments. Printed books, for the most part, were sold unbound, in sheets as they came from the press, so some Stationers' shops carried a selection of binding materials and decorations. Until the nineteenth century, England was a net importer from Continental Europe of both printed books and blank printing paper. Thus, many Stationers' stock included a high proportion of imported books. Stationers might also act as wholesale distributors of books in London, the English provinces, Continental Europe, or the American colonies.

53
Thomas Chard.
Letters and booklists, 1583–84,
to Thomas Bradshawe, Cambridge bookseller.
X.d. 168

These letters, written in 1583 and discovered in the binding of a book published in 1593, document the sale of books outside of London. Thomas Chard, at the sign of the Helmet in Paul's Cross Churchyard, specialized in import-ed theological works. Thomas Bradshaw was a bookbinder and bookseller in Cambridge. Chard and Bradshaw had both apprenticed in London with Humphrey Toy. Toy imported books wholesale from the Antwerp book entrepreneur Christopher Plantin and trained Chard and Bradshaw how to conduct business in the same way. The Continental books dis-cussed in the letters are predominantly theo-logical titles and devotional books, such as the Psalms. The books are identified by size, by special features such as being printed on vel-lum, having covers with clasps, or gilt edges, and they are priced.

54
The Following Collection or, Pious little treatises.
Douai, Michael Mairesse, 1684.
Book in sheets
Wing F1401.5

This collection of Roman Catholic devotions was printed by the English Catholic College at Douai, France, in the latter days of Charles II's reign. It would have been shipped to England in loose sheets, then folded and cut into pages when bound. Generally the purchaser chose his or her own binder. This book is remarkable because it is one of only two known copies and was never bound.

55
Catalogus universalis pro nundinis Francofurten-sibus autumnalibus, de anno M.DC.XIX.
London, Ex officina Nortoniana, apud Ioannem Billium, [1619].
Sigs. L1v–L2r
STC 11328

The sale of books by catalogue, and thus long distance sales, developed around the semi-annual fair in Frankfurt am Main, an early printing center. The first Frankfurt fair cata-logue was issued in 1564. In 1617, John Bill, a London book importer who shopped regularly at the fair, began printing a version of the catalogue in England. Bill's catalogue in Latin, using roman type, offered theological books first, as the largest category for sale. Also listed were law, medicine, politics, history, geography, philosophy, other humanities, music, and books printed in foreign languages. From 1622 to 1626 he included a section of books printed in English. Annotations on the last page of this text appear to be price calculations for the purchase or sale of a variety of books.

Der Buchhändler.
Sucht ihr der Weisheit Schatz: gebt gute Bücher Platz

Was ist des Menschen Leib alhier?
   ein Wander-Gut, auff alle Stunde
ein offt gedrucktes Papier;
   ein Buch, in Trübsal eingebunden,
mit diesem handelt Tod und Zeit,
bis einst auspackt die Ewigkeit.

56
Jan Luyken (1649–1712).
Engraving, from Christoph Weigel (1654–1725).
Abbildung der Germain-Nützlichen
Hauptstande von denen Regeten und ihren
so in Friedens.
Regensburg, 1698.
Plate preceding sig. Hh
Acc. 203725

A bookhandler, or wholesaler, supervises the packing of books. Both bound and unbound books were wrapped in bales, then packed into barrels for shipment. This method was employed from the medieval period and proved quite effective in preventing damage to books shipped long distances and by sea. Here a Continental bookseller holds an inventory, which he is checking against the bales being packed into the barrel.

57
Venterus Mandey and Joseph Moxon.
Mechanick-powers: or, the mistery of nature
and art unvail'd.
London, Printed for the authors, 1696.
Sigs. SS2v–SS3r
Wing M418

In the back of this book, co-authored, co-printed, and co-published by Joseph Moxon, is an advertisement for books and other items available in his shop "at the Sign of Atlas in Warwick-Lane, London." The list includes flat maps, maps for covering globes, and globes, all engraved, printed, built, and sold by Moxon. He also sold mathematical instruments. Moxon assures the reader that these products are available "at the lowest prices."

58
Jan Phoonsen (1631–1702).
Les Loix et les Coutumes du change des
Principales Places de l'Europe.
Amsterdam, Aux Depens d'Estienne Roger, 1715.
Frontispiece
Acc. 233513

The Dutch Republic was an international center for the book trade in the seventeenth century and had long welcomed foreign printers and booksellers. The freedom afforded by a Protestant territory not subject to the strictures of state and church censorship was attractive to many Europeans. This Dutch engraving provides some idea of the appearance of Continental bookshops. The shops of François l'Honoré and Jacques Desbordes, Walloon booksellers in Amsterdam, were on the ground floor of houses that fronted the Bourse, or Exchange. L'Honoré and Desbordes specialized in French books, particularly those banned in France.

59
Wenceslaus Hollar (1607–1677).
The portraicture of the most illustrious and
noble, William of Nassau, Prince of Orange, etc.
[London], Are to be sold by Tho. Ienner at the Old Exchange, [1641?].
Art Box H737.5 no. 19

60
Wenceslaus Hollar (1607–1677).
London.
[London, Printed by J. Streater, for H. Twiford, 1657].
Map L85a no. 1 copy 2

The most important bookshops in London were those encircling the northeast corner of St. Paul's Cathedral Churchyard. Avid readers would have been familiar with this area, also known as Paul's Cross Churchyard, or simply the Cross Yard. Along the north side of that space, a range of nearly three hundred feet, lay a continuous row of seventeen shops occupying the ground floors of three- and four-story buildings.

61
Peter W. M. Blayney.
Model of The Three Pigeons.
1998.
Generously lent by Peter W. M. Blayney

One of the largest and best-known of the Paul's bookshops bore the sign of The Judith until 1547, The Holy Ghost between 1548 and 1613, and The Three Pigeons from 1614 until at least 1684. This model (built by Peter W. M. Blayney for a 1998 lecture on the Paul's bookshops) is based on a description of 1656 and a survey of 1670. The unpainted two-story building beside and beneath The Three Pigeons is another bookshop, The Green Dragon.

Three Pigeons Books

During the time The Three Pigeons operated in Paul's Churchyard, it was occupied by at least four different Stationers. The first was William Barrett, who changed the name in 1614 from The Holy Ghost (represented on the sign by one white bird) to The Three Pigeons (represented on the sign by three white birds). Around 1620 John Parker became identified with the shop. The longest tenancy was that of Humphrey Robinson, who was there from at least 1627 until his death in 1670, having rebuilt after the Great Fire of 1666. John Baker II leased the shop from Robinson's heir until 1684.

This sample of books actually sold at The Three Pigeons ranges in size from folio to duodecimo. The smaller formats, which were cheaper to produce, dominate the selection.

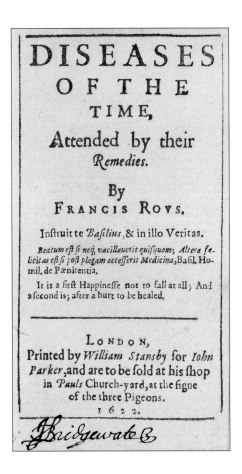

Rarer are the more expensive folio volumes like the Beaumont and Fletcher collected plays which Robinson published in partnership with Humphrey Moseley. Robinson occasionally partnered with Octavian Pulleyn, two doors down at the sign of The Rose, a primary supplier of books to the Bodleian Library of Oxford University.

Both church and state viewed the freedom to read as dangerous because it led to diversity of thought and multiplicity of opinion, inspiring heresy and rebellion. States since ancient Athens had tried to limit available reading materials. The Roman Catholic Church had been a particularly active censor, burning and banning books. Licenses to publish were also instituted. In the era of printing, pre-publication licensing proved most effective, but controls could be eluded by subterfuge, moving production to a more lenient jurisdiction, or resorting to a medium more difficult to police, such as manuscript.

62

Great Britain.
Laws, statutes, etc., 1509–1547 (Henry VIII).
Anno tricesimo quarto et quinto Herici [*sic*]
Octavi.
Actes made in the session of this present parlyment.
London, In Fletestrete, in the house of
Thomas Barthelet, [1543?].
Sig. Aivr
STC 9407.2

Rethinking the English Reformation toward the end of his life, Henry VIII placed restrictions on reading and printing. In 1543 this act of Parliament resolved that no one was to read the Bible publicly without the king's permission. Only noble and gentle MEN were permitted to read the Bible aloud to their households. Women of the same social standing were allowed to read only silently to themselves. To prevent "naughty and erroneous opinions" among the lower classes, both genders were forbidden to read the Bible aloud. This same act prohibited the printing of "pestiferous" religious texts, including William Tyndale's English Bible, and called for hand alterations of copies already printed.

63

Index librorum prohibitorum . . . Clementis Papae VIII.
Paris, Apud Laurentium Sonnium, 1599.
Sig. Giir
Z 1020 1599a Cage

The Propaganda Index was institutionalized by the Roman Catholic Church in the sixteenth century as a tool of the Counter-Reformation. It was intended to encourage the reading of 'good' books and to discourage the reading of books that might corrupt morals or faith. This edition from 1599 banned the works of King Henry VIII of England. Three pages later, however, his early writing attacking Martin Luther and defending the Catholic Church (which had earned Henry the title 'Defender of the Faith' before his adoption of Protestantism), was excepted from the ban.

64

Vox Spiritus, or Sr. Walter Rawleigh's Ghoste.
Manuscript, ca. 1625.
Title page
V.a. 223

The original manuscript of this work was confiscated from the author, the Jacobean news writer Captain Thomas Gainsford, during a 1621 government raid. A politically controversial text, it never achieved print, but it circulated widely in manuscript. Manuscript editions like this one were copied by professional scribes and sold by Stationers, to the chagrin of the government. A vigorous reading audience encouraged this type of surreptitious manuscript publication. This manuscript was preserved over time but bears no evidence of the readers' engagement with the text. Illicit texts possibly were considered too dangerous to annotate.

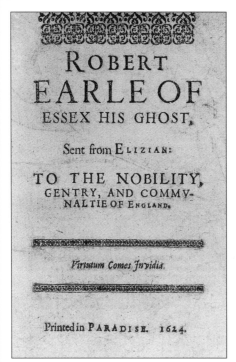

ROBERT
EARLE OF
ESSEX HIS GHOST,

Sent from ELIZIAN:

TO THE NOBILITY,
GENTRY, AND COMMV-
NALTIE OF ENGLAND.

Virtutum Comes Invidia.

Printed in PARADISE. 1624.

65

65
[Thomas Scott] (1580?–1626).
Robert Earle of Essex his ghost.
Printed in Paradise [i.e. London], 1624.
Title page
STC 22084a copy 1

The imprint lists "Paradise" as the place of
publication, but this political polemic was
almost certainly printed illegally in London.
Fictional locations were used to protect
printers and/or publishers from potential
prosecution by the English government. By
1624 the author, Thomas Scott (not named
on the title page), was a controversial figure.
He had run afoul of the authorities regulating
printing with his criticism of James I's foreign
and religious policy (see cat. nos. 8–10 above).
It was extremely unlikely that Scott's
works would have been approved by the
pre-publication licensing process.

66
William Prynne (1600–1669).
*Hidden workes of darkenes [sic] brought
to publike light.*
London, Printed by T. Brudenell for
M. Sparke, Senior, 1645.
Frontispiece
Wing P3973 bound with P3904

Hollar's detailed etching of the 1644 trial
of William Laud, archbishop of Canterbury
(figure A), includes a table covered with
altered and banned books. Among other
offenses, Laud was charged with preventing
publication of good Protestant books,
instead allowing 'popish' books to be printed.
Witnesses at the trial included authors
William Prynne (G), Henry Burton (H), and
Prynne's publisher, Michael Sparke, Sr. (S),
all of whom had suffered at the hands of
Laud when he was in charge of ecclesiastical
pre-publication licensing. Laud was ultimately
convicted of treason and executed.

67
Guilielmus Antonius Saldenus (1627–1694).
De Libris Varioque eorum usu & abusu.
Amsterdam, Ex officina Henrici and viduae
Theodori Boom, 1688.
Engraved title page
Z1003 S3 1688 Cage copy 1

This allegorical scene presents a spectrum of
responses to books. On the left are represented
positive attitudes. A scholar clad in gown and
soft slippers (*hac delector*) delights in books.
Through the window arch behind him, an
orderly group of people enter a church with
godly books in hand. Negative attitudes are
represented by the stern-faced, standing man
with a sword (*hanc aversor*) on the right.
Through the window behind him a disorderly
mob throws books into a blazing fire.

LIBRARIA
SUPELLE

HANC
ÆSTIMOR

HAC DELECTOR

GUILJELMUS SALDENUS
de
LIBRIS
Varioque eorum
USU et ABUSU
LIBRI II.

Joh. vanden Aveele, jun. fecit.

67

'His mind and hand went together': The Reader's Hand

Readers relate to books not only with their eyes, but also with their hands. Hands select a book from the shelf, hold it open for reading, and mark the reader's place in the pages. The reader's hand manipulates the pen, expressing a wide range of responses to texts. So integral was the hand to reading that it evolved as a characteristic written and printed symbol highlighting specific passages in both manuscript and printed texts.

68
Annibale Carracci (1560–1609).
Diverse figure al numero di ottanta.
Rome, Nella stamperia Lodovico Grigniani,
[1646].
Plate 44
NC 1155 C3 D5 1646 Cage

Annibale Carracci, a member of the renowned Bolognese family of artists, portrayed a variety of common trades, including the traveling bookseller. Traveling booksellers made books more accessible to readers in rural areas, especially to women who might not frequent urban shops. He holds an open book reading as he walks, perhaps as a sales pitch. Hornbooks dangling from the rim of his basket were intended to catch a mother's eye and the man-uscript caption explains that the bookseller's wares were to be read by children.

69
Aristotle.
Physica (and eleven other works).
Manuscript, ca. 1300.
Fols. 197v–198r
V.b. 32
Illustrated on page 18.

Human presence has been riotously interjected into this manuscript by the scribe's hand. He has cleverly expanded decoration typical of the gothic page both to assist and allure the reader. Pointing hands with prominent index fingers connect marginal comments to the main text. The hands are enhanced by drawings of a lion's head and a caricatured human head. An initial *N* shelters horses' heads while an initial *O* encircles a face resembling a court jester.

70
Boethius (d. 524). *Auitij Maulij Torquati Seuerini Boetij ordinarij patricij viri exconsulis De consolatione.*
[Nuremberg], Anthonij Koburgers ciuis inclite Nurnberge[n]siu[m] vrbis Industria fabrefactus, [1483].
Sigs. diiiv–diiiir
INC B694

Minimal punctuation in this early printed edition of an influential philosophical work necessitated the addition of hand-colored rubrication and handwritten annotations to guide the reader. Among the marginalia, pointing hands highlight part of the text. Beside the red and blue painted initials, an annotator has drawn a pointing hand, a human skull, and written "*Mors,*" the Latin word for death. Elsewhere, an additional ¶ (paragraph mark) has been added in black ink. Multiple hands, of the scribe, the rubricator, and the reader, have clearly shaped this text.

71
Sir John Harington (1561–1612).
Epigrams.
Manuscript, 1605.
Fol. 122
V.a. 249

Harington's manuscript book of epigrams was created for the adolescent Prince Henry, James I's heir. This verse satirizes a former priest enumerating on his fingers the "com-modities" of marriage. The four fingers of the hand, drawn in the margin, represent wife, friends, money, and children. Some are "firm" and some "flee," leaving only wife and children,

Tavolette, e Libri per li putti.
Primmer or Books for Children

68

as suggested by the bottom illustration of two fingers in the shape of 'horns.' The drawing reveals that the unworldly ex-priest has been cuckolded by his wife and that the children are not his. In this manuscript, the hand conveys human expression on a number of levels.

72

John Brinsley, (fl. 1633).
Ludus literarius: or, the grammar schoole.
London, Printed for Thomas Man, 1612.
Sigs. F2v–F3r
STC 3768 copy 1

Written by one of Charles I's childhood tutors, this textbook for teachers in "poore Countrey schooles" taught reading first, then writing. A chapter entitled "Directions for faire writing" addresses proper penmanship. By holding the pen correctly and practicing certain strokes and "rude flourishes," students could produce beautiful script. The importance of these instructions was emphasized by pointing hands, in elegant lace cuffs, printed in the margin. Later editions were aimed at "the inferiour sort" in Ireland, Virginia, and the Somers Islands.

73

John Stow (1525?–1605).
A survey of London.
London, By Iohn Wolfe, 1598.
Sigs. Aa6v– Aa7r
STC 23341 copy 2

Distinctive pointing hands, characterized by black-tipped thumbs, litter the margins of Stow's description of London neighborhoods. The hands point to passages significant to former owner John Gibbon. A post-Restoration antiquary and herald, Gibbon used this book to research history, heraldry, and to make contributions to Strype's early-eighteenth-century revision of Stow. A notorious annotator of books (his own and others'), Gibbon drew pictures of existing buildings in the margins. This cosmopolitan great-granduncle of historian Edward Gibbon (author of *The Decline and Fall of the Roman Empire*) also recorded important personal events in this volume, like his appointment to office and the death of his wife.

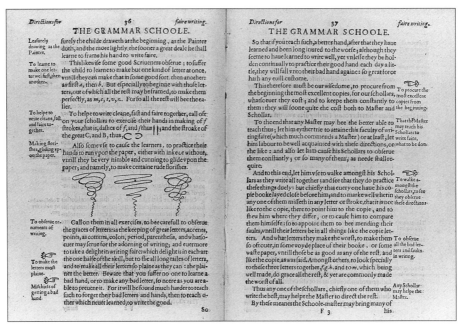

72

In manuscripts, addresses to the reader ("Ad Lectorum") developed along with instructive symbols such as rubrication and manicules to guide interpretation of the text. In printed books, words alone were favored by printers, publishers, fans, detractors, or virtually anyone to influence the reader. By the eighteenth century, this practice had become standardized as the preface, without which a book was considered incomplete.

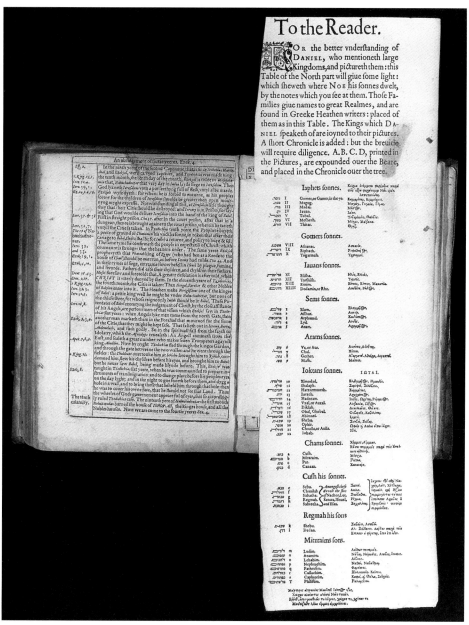

74

74
Hugh Broughton (1549–1612).
A concert of scripture.
London, [By Richard Watkins] for Gabriell
Simson and William White,
[between 1587 and 1591].
Fold-out tipped-in between D4v and E1r
STC 3850 copy 2 bound with STC 3853 copy 2

These instructions to the reader are unusually
located, inserted midway through a controversial religious text. A preface at the beginning
of the book, citing the example of Mosaic law
read in the Temple, is full of instructions on how
readers should interpret the cross references,
tables, abbreviations, and annotations in this
work. Written by an outspoken minister,
who regularly preached on the subject, this
chronology of biblical events is also illustrated
with numerous diagrams, pictures, and maps.

75
William Lily (1468?–1522).
*A short Introduction of grammar . . .
Compiled . . . for . . . all those that intend to
attaine the knowledge of the Latin tongue.*
[Paris, By Conrad Badius], 1557.
Sigs. aiv–aiir
STC 15612 copy 1

Authorized by Henry VIII in 1540, this school-
book included multiple prefaces to the reader.
In the first, in miniscule roman type, "THE
PRINTER WISHETH THE FEARE OF God to
all Ouersears and Instructers of youth." In the
second, the author offers "AN ADVERTISE-
MENT to the Reader" explaining use of the
apostrophe in the Latin and Greek text. The
third, in the largest type, filling an entire page,
makes a pitch for the teaching method out-
lined in this book to become standard. The
author's preface succeeded beyond his wildest
expectations: Lily's *Grammar* went into at least
fifty identifiable editions before 1640.

76
William Shakespeare (1564–1616).
*Mr. William Shakespeare's comedies, histories
and tragedies.*
London, By Isaac Iaggard and Ed. Blount, 1623.
Sig. A3r
STC 22273 no. 9

The prefatory material to Shakespeare's
First Folio includes this address "To the
Great Variety of Readers." In it, Heminge and
Condell extoll the virtues of the author's work
and the quality of this book, in the hope of
stimulating sales. They also recommend the
four memorial poems following their preface
as a guide to readers. The poems are followed
by an "Epistle dedicatorie" commending
William (cat. no. 80) and Philip Herbert,
"the most noble and incomparable paire of
brethren," for their patronage.

77
Edward Coote (fl. 1597).
The English school-master.
[London], By A. Maxwell for the Company
of Stationers, 1670.
Sigs. L3v–L4r
Wing C6073

This unique volume was intended for teaching
tradesmen's apprentices and young children to
read and write. The "To the Reader" address
explains that the book may be divided in half.
The first part was designed to teach rudimentary reading skills to beginners. The "fairer"
pages of the second part were aimed at teaching
more advanced reading skills and writing.
Reflecting the book's sixteenth-century origins
and the handwriting practices of that time,
the alphabet, vowels, syllables, and a prayer
follow in secretary script, providing examples
to be copied. The organization of this much-
reprinted textbook shows that reading and
writing were taught independently, and that
reading was taught first.

To the great Variety of Readers.

FRom the moſt able, to him that can but ſpell: There you are number'd. We had rather you were weighd. Eſpecially, when the fate of all Bookes depends vpon your capacities : and not of your heads alone, but of your purſes. Well ! It is now publique, & you wil ſtand for your priuiledges wee know : to read, and cenſure. Do ſo, but buy it firſt. That doth beſt commend a Booke, the Stationer ſaies. Then, how odde ſoeuer your braines be, or your wiſedomes, make your licence the ſame, and ſpare not. Iudge your ſixe-pen'orth, your ſhillings worth, your fiue ſhillings worth at a time, or higher, ſo you riſe to the iuſt rates, and welcome. But, what euer you do, Buy. Cenſure will not driue a Trade, or make the Iacke go. And though you be a Magiſtrate of wit, and ſit on the Stage at *Black-Friers*, or the *Cock-pit*, to arraigne Playes dailie, know, theſe Playes haue had their triall alreadie, and ſtood out all Appeales ; and do now come forth quitted rather by a Decree of Court, then any purchas'd Letters of commendation.

It had bene a thing, we confeſſe, worthie to haue bene wiſhed, that the Author himſelfe had liu'd to haue ſet forth, and ouerſeen his owne writings ; But ſince it hath bin ordain'd otherwiſe, and he by death departed from that right, we pray you do not envie his Friends, the office of their care, and paine, to haue collected & publiſh'd them ; and ſo to haue publiſh'd them, as where (before) you were abus'd with diuerſe ſtolne, and ſurreptitious copies, maimed, and deformed by the frauds and ſtealthes of iniurious impoſtors, that expos'd them : euen thoſe, are now offer'd to your view cur'd, and perfect of their limbes ; and all the reſt, abſolute in their numbers, as he conceiued thē. Who, as he was a happie imitator of Nature, was a moſt gentle expreſſer of it. His mind and hand went together : And what he thought, he vttered with that eaſineſſe, that wee haue ſcarſe receiued from him a blot in his papers. But it is not our prouince, who onely gather his works, and giue them you, to praiſe him. It is yours that reade him. And there we hope, to your diuers capacities, you will finde enough, both to draw, and hold you : for his wit can no more lie hid, then it could be loſt. Reade him, therefore ; and againe, and againe : And if then you doe not like him, ſurely you are in ſome manifeſt danger, not to vnderſtand him. And ſo we leaue you to other of his Friends, whom if you need, can bee your guides : if you neede them not, you can leade your ſelues, and others. And ſuch Readers we wiſh him.

A 3   *Iohn Heminge.*
             Henrie Condell.

76

78
William Cartwright (1611–1643).
Comedies, tragi-comedies, with other poems.
London, Printed for H. Moseley, 1651.
Sigs. ***11v–***12r
Wing C709 copy 2 vol. 1

Humphrey Moseley, a bookseller in Paul's
Cross Churchyard, saw this collected edition
of Cartwright's plays and poetry through the
press. The reader had to wade through fifty-
four commemorative poems before reading
a word of the author's devising. The last poem
was by Moseley himself. He followed it with
a "Postscript" explaining production delays
and other faults, including the absence of an
index because the book was too thick already.
He emphasized that any mistakes found must
have been made by the printer since Cartwright's
manuscripts, personally prepared by Moseley,
were perfect.

79
William Cockburn (1669–1739).
*Profluvia ventris: or, the nature and causes
of loosenesses.*
London, Printed for B. Barker and G. Strahan,
1701.
Sig. A2r
Acc. 190-067q

In his bluntly titled "THE PREFACE," the
author of this medical text explains that
custom dictates its inclusion. A book without
a preface is like "a Minister without his
Credentials." The author views this obligation
as a hardship, yet one he feels compelled to
endure. Cockburn was a physician world-
renowned for his cure for dysentery contracted
by sailors and soldiers. He published a number
of tedious medical works, apparently uninfect-
ed by the literary inclinations of one of his
more famous patients, Jonathan Swift.

80
Isaac Oliver (1556?–1617).
William Herbert, third Earl of Pembroke.
Oval miniature, 1611.
Watercolor with bodycolor on vellum
FPm10

81
David Loggan (1635–1700?).
Exterior and interior views of the buildings
at Oxford and the University.
London, n.d.
Etchings
Art file O98.6 nos. 24 and 25

Founded in the fourteenth century, the
Oxford University Library is one of the oldest
in Europe. Refounded in 1598 by Sir Thomas
Bodley, a former diplomat, the Bodleian
Library opened for the "public use" of Oxford
students on 8 November 1602. Shown here are
the Arts End (east view) and the Selden End
(west view), built to accommodate growth of
the collection during the seventeenth century.
The Selden End is filled with important
contemporary bequests. Shelves on the ground
level house the eponymous books and manuscripts of lawyer and antiquary, John Selden.
On the mezzanine are bequests from Sir
Kenelm Digby, an alchemy scholar; Archbishop
William Laud, chancellor of the University,
1630–1645; and William Herbert, third earl
of Pembroke. In 1629 Pembroke presented the
Library with a collection of over 250 manuscript works on numerous topics and in
various languages. He preceded Laud as
chancellor of the University from 1617 until
his death in 1630.

Throughout the seventeenth century, the community of readers grew and became more inclusive. One factor in this growth was the call for increased and improved education for women. Another factor was the agricultural revolution which afforded children and laborers more educational opportunities. The resulting improvement in literacy rates among previously marginal groups increased the demand for, and contributed to the proliferation of, lower-priced reading materials. Predictably, quantity provoked concerns about quality.

82

John, of Garland (ca. 1195–ca. 1272).
Synonima.
London, Impressus per me Winandum de
Worde, 1505.
Sigs. Pxiiv–a1r
STC 11614 bound with STC 23185

Schoolbooks have always been among the most susceptible to damage and destruction by their readers, as evidenced by these defaced pages. The schoolboy drawing of a man in a cap, holding a long rod and pointing his finger mocks the smiling image of a schoolmaster in the woodcut opposite. Among the scribbles is an ownership inscription of "Temys a Sydnah[a]m," perhaps the artist. This unique volume contains eleven Latin grammars published by Wynkyn de Worde. The initials "WC" were the printer's device of De Worde's father-in-law, William Caxton, first printer in England.

82

83
Juan Luis Vives (1492–1540).
De officio mariti.
Augspurg [*sic*], Bey Hainrich Stayner, 1544.
Sigs. aaivv–A1r
PA 8588 D4 1544 Cage

Written by a renowned early-sixteenth-century
Spanish humanist, this treatise promoting
women's education was widely disseminated
throughout Europe. Commissioned by
Catherine of Aragon, first wife of Henry VIII,
for their daughter Mary Tudor, Vives's book
portrays Isabella of Castile, Mary's grand-
mother and Catherine's mother, as the female
role-model. Queen Isabella fought her half-
brother for the throne and, independent of the
wishes of her husband King Ferdinand and
her advisors, funded Columbus's voyage to
America. In apparent contradiction, Vives
concluded that women, despite their education and capabilities, should still choose only
the traditional female life-roles: chaste virgin,
virtuous wife and mother, and pious widow.

84
Arthur Dent (1553?–1601).
*A sermon of repentaunce . . . 1581 . . .
the 7. of March.*
London, for Iohn Harison, 1583.
Title page
STC 6652

85
Richard Sibbes (1577–1635).
The soules conflict with It selfe. . . .
3d edition.
London, By M. F. for R. Dawlman, 1636.
Binding and front pastedown
STC 22510

The use of printed labels to signify ownership
emerged among Elizabethan university students
in imitation of more aristocratic collectors.
Other groups of readers later adopted this
practice. The unidentified William Nordan
was likely university-educated. Ownership of
this very popular Puritan sermon may indicate

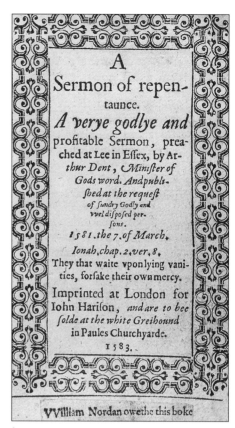

84

85

religious inclination, or that he was a cleric
himself. 'Oweth' was a common usage for
'owneth' in this period.

Anne Lake is one of only ten Englishwomen
known to have used printed book labels prior
to 1650. Her initials are also stamped on the
covers of the custom binding. Nothing else is
known about this mysterious female owner.

DIVINITY   MORALITY

HISTORY POETRY PHYSICK

SURGERY

Sturt sc:

The Excellent Woman

Printed for Joseph Watts

86

86
[Jaques Du Bosc] (d. 1660).
The excellent woman.
London, For Joseph Watts, 1692.
Engraved title page
Acc. 225972

The English translation of *L'honneste femme* was dedicated to Lady Mary Walcot, represented figuratively, if not literally, in the frontispiece. The book was intended to assist women in distinguishing virtue from vice in themselves and in the world. Virtue, a highly desirable quality in women, could be obtained and improved through reading. The translator advocated that reading should be taught to all women—"the larger Half of Mankind"—regardless of status. If nothing else, well-educated and knowledgeable women might have a positive influence on the actions of men.

87
Elegantiores praestantium vitorum satyrae.
Lugduni Batavorum, Ex officina Joannis Maire, 1655.
Engraved title page
PN 6154 E5 Cage vol. 1

A reader peruses a volume recommended to him by a bookseller in the form of a satyr. Traditionally, the figure of the satyr represented the literary genre of satire, which exposes human folly to public view. The satyr also symbolized disapproval, evident in his obvious disdain for the reader's indiscriminant taste.

88
John Gay (1685–1732).
Fables.
London, For W. Strahan, J. and F. Rivington [etc.], 1769.
Plate: Fable 10
Acc. 167874

Gay's anthropomorphic nursery rhymes portray an elephant reading. The bookseller, noting his client's wisdom and insight, offers to employ the elephant as an author. The

88

elephant refuses, preferring to remain a reader, leaving authorship to "the senseless sons of men." Written by the social-climbing Gay in hopes of attaining a royal post, the *Fables* were dedicated to four-year-old William, duke of Cumberland, and provided a commentary on the quality of what people were reading. Gay's *Fables* became a popular children's classic and were printed in more than 350 editions before 1890. Today, however, Gay is best known for his *Beggar's Opera.*

Early modern readers identified with their books on many levels. Some viewed them as almost mystical, as objects to be revered and passed on to future generations. Many owners decorated their books with custom bindings, gauffered gilt edges, and other ornamentation. Thus made beautiful, they became icons, valued perhaps as much for external appearance as for internal content, although it was frequently the Bible that was objectified in this manner. The range of sentiments expressed by readers transformed ordinary books into valued keepsakes.

89
Bible. English. 1580. Geneva version.
The Bible translated according to the Ebrew and Greeke.
London, Christopher Barker, 1580.
Binding
STC 2129

Frances Newby, one owner of this Bible, crafted an enduring relationship with it. On an endleaf at the back of the volume, Frances recorded: "My ffather Samuell: Newby gaue me this booke ye 7ᵗʰ of october 1644—wth a charch [charge] to keep it as long as I liue — F:N:" The following year, Frances commissioned a custom binding reflecting his commitment to this charge. Stamped on the front cover is: "FRANCES NEWBY HIS | BOOK GIVEN HIM BY," and on the back cover: "HIS FATHER SAMVELL | NEWBY 1645."

90
Esther Inglis (1571–1624).
Augumenta psalmorum Davidis . . . Henrico oblato.
Manuscript, 1608.
Binding
V.a. 94
The Gift of Lessing J. Rosenwald

Splendidly bound in red velvet embroidered with silver thread and seed pearls, this book is fit for a king. Latin paraphrases of the Psalms in beautiful and precise script are illuminated in brilliant colors. Calligrapher Esther Inglis (see cat. nos. 4 and 5) created this manuscript and binding to attract an elite patron.

Completed in 1608, the volume is dedicated to, and was probably presented to Henry, Prince of Wales, heir to the English throne until his untimely death in 1612. While there is no direct evidence of ownership or readership of this book, its beauty insured its survival.

91
Bible. N.T. English. Geneva Version.
The new testament . . . Englished by L. Tomson.
London, Robert Barker, 1609.
With
Bible. O.T. Psalms. English. Paraphrases. 1610.
The whole booke of Psalmes.
London, Printed for the Companie of Stationers, 1610.
Dos-à-dos binding
STC 2907 bound with STC 2535.2

A series of literate and talented women owned this New Testament and book of Psalms in a seventeenth-century dos-à-dos binding. In 1661, Elizabeth Crewe wrote on an endleaf: "the gift of my grandmother | Jones to my mother, & my | mothers gift to me." On the white satin cover is embroidered the Tudor rose watered by silver-spangled rain from the brilliant blue clouds above and below. The edges of the pages were gilt and gauffered. A nineteenth-century owner, Elizabeth Heinzelmann, valued this volume enough to write her name on an endleaf of the Psalms.

92

92
Sir Edward Dering, bart. (1598–1644).
A collection of speeches made by Sir Edward Dering.
London, By E. G. for F. Eglesfield, and Jo. Stafford, 1642.
Binding
Wing D1104

As a member of the Long Parliament's committee to regulate printing, Sir Edward Dering was well-aware of the power of print and apparently, the force of iconography. This gold-stamped vellum binding displays Dering's crest, a Kentish horse, in a field of fleur-de-lis. It adorns a printed edition of Dering's writings, introduced by an oversized, fold-out portrait of the author himself. The title page of this vanity volume is inscribed with the name of Dering's third wife, Unton, and that of Henry English, another relation.

due to heavy use, and stamped decoration has been almost worn away. Still barely visible is a pelican, believed to pierce its breast to feed its young, symbolizing the redemptive power of Christ's blood, here extended to his words.

94
Bible. O.T. Psalms. English. Paraphrases. 1639.
The whole booke of Psalmes: collected into English meter.
London, By I. L. for the Company of Stationers, 1639.
Binding
STC 2689 copy 1

David, the archetypal underdog, graces the exquisitely embroidered binding on this *Book of Psalms*, a work that he authored as King of Israel. Although lavishly decorated, this book has no internal markings or other evidence of its readers.

93

93
[John Taylor] (1580–1653).
Verbum sempiternum.
Part II: Salvator Mvndi
London, By Io. Beale, 1631.
Dos-à-dos Binding
STC 23811.2

John Taylor, the water poet, authored this 'thumb Bible,' a miniature verse adaptation of Scripture. Internal inscriptions reveal that Leighton Owen owned this book for at least twenty years in the mid-seventeenth century. Once beautiful, the goatskin dos-à-dos binding has faded from its original pink or red color

Marginalia open an important window into the past lives of both books and readers, often revealing the innermost thoughts of those long dead and little known. Manuscript annotations in early modern books encompass a wide range of human experience and emotion. This interaction evidences a deeper level of personal involvement between book and reader—from humorous to grave, from inane to practical.

95
Desiderius Erasmus (d. 1536).
De duplici copia verborum.
London, Excudebat Sibertus Roedius, 1556.
Sig. X4v
STC 10471.8

On the verso of the last page, a former owner has written: "Edmond Trott his booke Amen Whomsoever findeth this book let him restore it to the oner hee shall be well paid for his paines." Offering a reward for the return of his book indicates that Trott considered it valuable, whether due to its cost or its content. Other marks of ownership include the name of "Mr. Anthony Watson" and a monogram on the title page. Internal manuscript annotations, some in Greek, show that this book was used by its many readers.

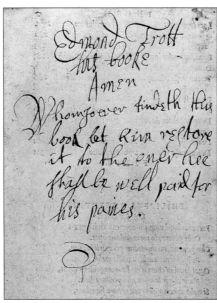

95

96
Bible. N.T. Latin. 1568. Erasmus.
Testamentum novum.
London, Apud Gerardum Dewes, 1568.
Sig. Dd7v
STC 2800 copy 1

In this New Testament, a reader or readers heavily annotated the book of Acts. On the last page, an early owner, William Hill, wrote a poem describing his father's gift of the book to him with the admonition that he should learn from its content. Over the centuries, numerous owners have left their marks in this Latin translation by Erasmus printed in England.

97
Great Britain. Laws, statutes, etc.,
1603–1625 (James I).
Anno regni Iacobi Regis Angliae Scotiae, Franciae.
London, By Bonham Norton and Iohn Bill, 1624.
Sigs. H5v–H6r
STC 9507

A lawyer, who was also a judge, heavily annotated his copy of early Stuart statutes, using Law French. This 1624 Act of Parliament criminalized infanticide, in particular murder of bastard children to conceal adultery or fornication. The judge obviously used his book for many years, recording opinions in cases he heard, including some infanticide trials held at Newgate Prison. He noted circumstances surrounding the surreptitious delivery and murder of babies as well as the sentences handed down in various cases.

Matth. 3.	ligant, *& conuertantur, & sanem eos. No-
Psal. 66.	tum ergo sit vobis, *quòd gentibus missum
Esa. 11. 41.	est hoc salutare Dei, & ipsi audient. Et cùm
60.	hæc dixisset, exierunt ab eo Iudæi, multam
Hier. 16.	habentes inter se disceptationem. Mansit
& 31.	autem Paulus biennio toto in suo conductu,
Iohel. 3.	& suscipiebat omnes qui ingrediebantur ad ipsum, prædicans regnum
Malac. 1.	Dei, *ac docens quæ sunt de
Suprà 28.	Domino IESV cum

omni fiducia, ne-
mine prohi-
bente.

ACTORVM APOSTOLORVM FINIS.

IN

William Hill
is my name;
the right owner
of this same;
if I leaue it not
I am too blame;
for my father gaue
it mee to ye ende
because hee is m
dearest freind

96

98

Johann Gerhard (1582–1637).
*Gerard's meditations . . . Translated and revised
by Ralph Winterton . . .* 6th edition.
Cambridge, By R. Daniel, 1640.
Back endleaf
STC 11779

This popular book of prayers and meditations
bears the signature of Dorothy Charlton. She
was probably the mother of the many children
whose births she recorded on the back endleaves. Her regard for this book, perhaps the
only one she owned, made it an ideal place
to document important personal milestones.
Her chronicle gives some indication of an
early modern woman's life experiences, both
as a mother and a reader.

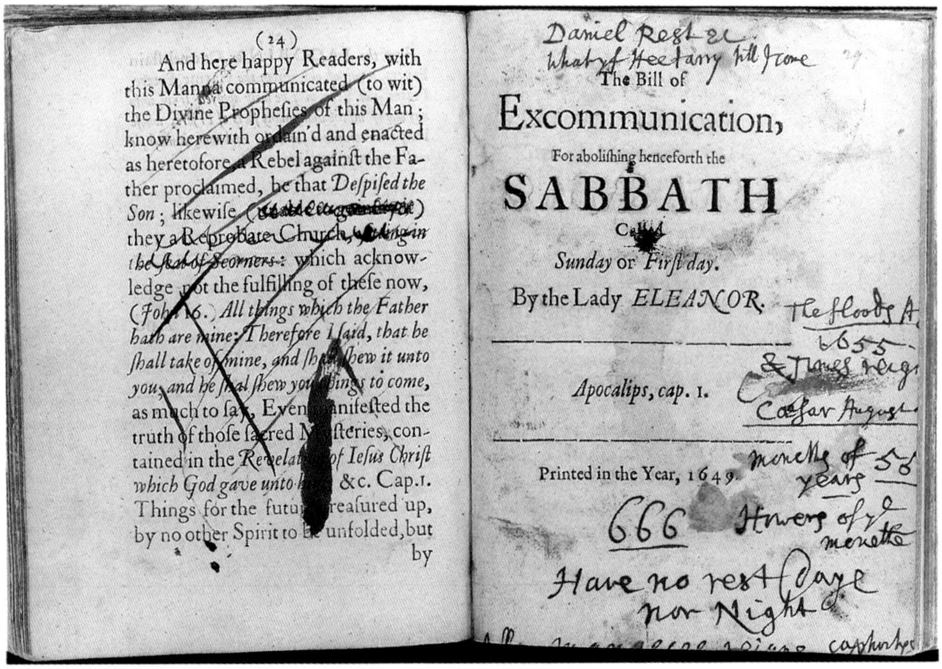

99

Lady Eleanor (Touchet) Davies Douglas (d. 1652).
Samson's fall (and 44 other titles).
London, Printed in the year 1642
[i.e. 1649].
Title page, *The Bill of Excommunication*
Wing D2010

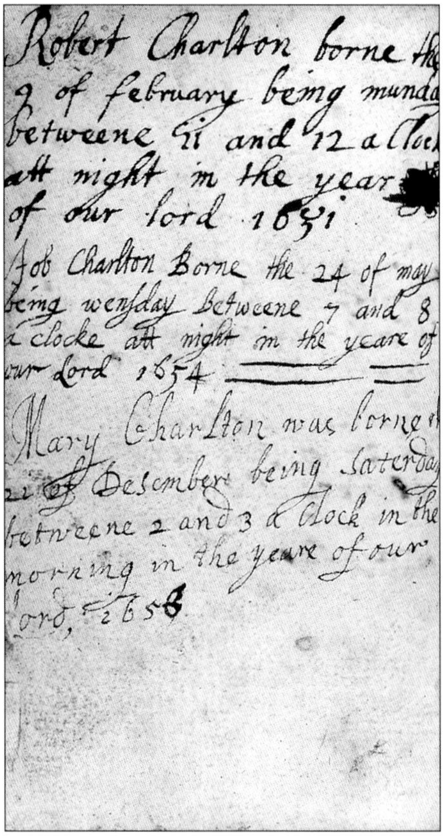

98

99

Contemporaries and historians alike are unsure whether Lady Eleanor Touchet Davies Douglas was the prophet she claimed to be, or merely mentally unstable, as she appeared to be. A woman of means, Lady Eleanor self-financed the illegal publication of her prophecies of impending doom. This collected volume belonged to the author, and later to one of her female relatives, the countess of Huntington. Lady Eleanor clearly had a lively interaction with her printed work, covering it in revisions, deletions, excisions, and amplifications.

100
Gilbert Burnet, bishop of Salisbury (1643–1715).
Some letters. Containing an account of what seemed most remarkable in Switzerland, Italy, &c.
Rotterdam, Printed by Abraham Archer, 1686.
Sigs. Cvv–Cvir
Wing B5915

High-profile changes of allegiance and tolerationist views made Gilbert Burnet, bishop of Salisbury, a controversial figure in the late-seventeenth century. One contemporary reader of Burnet's travel book clearly found its political and religious themes repugnant and voiced his disapproval of the author's views in his marginalia. Responding to Burnet's comments on Swiss religious differences, the reader argues: "This false Remark is the Author his chief design in all this Book." Controversy between author and reader, between text and margin, rages throughout the volume.

101
Commonplace Book.
Manuscript, ca. 1630.
Fol. (v)r
V.a. 345
Illustrated on page 44.

This manuscript collection of lyric poetry reveals the compiler's love of that genre. Assembled in the early-seventeenth century, most likely by a student at Christ Church, Oxford, it is an overt example of reading simply for the sheer joy and pleasure of doing so. The compiler clearly read many books of poetry, in manuscript and print, which he refashioned into books for his own enjoyment. Anticipating criticism of his passion, in verses "Ad Lectorum," he writes: " Some may perchance account my time misspent. . . . Yet some time must be spent in recreation."

III. Early Modern Readers Revealed Through Collecting and Preservation
'Rather soiled by use': Henry Clay Folger as a Collector of Marked Books

Henry Clay Folger assembled the collection that is the foundation of the Folger Shakespeare Library. By the early twentieth century, he had developed a reputation among book dealers for his interest in volumes containing marginalia. Many collectors preferred the cleanest, most pristine copies available, often inducing dealers to destroy manuscript markings through cutting, cropping, or bleaching. Mr. Folger's interest in marginalia has preserved for scholars a substantial body of evidence revealing the interests and practices of early modern readers.

102

Marcus Tullius Cicero
De oratore libri III.
Venice, Ex Bibliotheca Aldina [i.e. Haeredes Federici Torresani], 1569.
Sig. F8v
PA 6296 D6 1569 Cage
Illustrated on page 84.

The Aldine Press published this 1569 edition of Cicero's *Orations* purchased by Mr. Folger in 1927 from the English bookdealer N. M. Broadbent. Written on the last page is a key to an annotation system allegedly developed by Francis Bacon and Ben Jonson to mark their books. These symbols, found throughout the text, lent credence to Broadbent's theory of this book's distinguished provenance. However, the trefoil, or three-leaf clover, prominent among these symbols, was in fact a common motif, familiar from architectural and heraldic decoration. It occurs in marginalia written by a great variety of readers.

103

Marcus Tullius Cicero
De oratore libri III.
Frankfort, Excudebat Petrus Brubacchius, 1558.
Sigs. D6v–D7r
PA 6296 D6 1558 Cage

This 1558 edition of Cicero's *Orations* was also part of the Broadbent collection acquired by Folger. Broadbent believed that the marginalia in this volume were by Bacon and/or Jonson because they included symbols from the key in

the 1569 edition (cat. no. 102). Scholars have since determined that the handwriting is neither that of Jonson nor Bacon, nor the annotator of the 1569 Cicero. It may be that of William Wood, an early modern reader who wrote his name in this book.

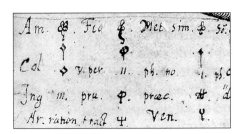

102 DETAIL

104

Marcus Valerius Martialis (ca. 40–ca. 104).
M. Val. Martialis nova editio.
Lugduni Batavorum, Apud Ioannem Maire, 1619.
Title page
PA 6501 A2 1619 Cage

On the title page of Martial's *Epigrams*, printed at Leiden in 1619, is written "*tanquam Explor[ator]*" and "*Sum Ben: Jonsonij*," Jonson's authentic motto and signature. Marginalia throughout the book include trefoils, brackets, pointing hands, and underlining. Jonson also noted cross-references to other epigrams and texts; allegories that could be applied to contemporary acquaintances such as Inigo Jones; and a number of instances where he believed Martial wrote about fellatio. There is little doubt that this volume was owned, read, and annotated by the great poetaster himself.

105
Aristotle.
Aristotelis de natura animalium libri nouem.
[Venice], Iohannes & Gregorius de Gregoriis, [18 Nov.] 1492.
Sigs. bivv–bvr
INC A871

In 1924, Folger purchased from W. T. Smedley a collection that included numerous books with marginalia. Among them was this edition of *The Nature of Animals*, printed during Columbus's first voyage to America. Annotated in fine humanist script, using black and red ink, the margins display brackets, comments, and pointing hands linking text and annotations, but no trefoils. The handwriting suggests that these marks were made too early to be those of Francis Bacon, as Smedley believed.

106
N. M. Broadbent.
Letter to Joseph Quincy Adams, Supervisor of Research of the Folger Shakespeare Library.
9 July 1931.
Folger Archives, Broadbent folder

Over the years, Henry Clay Folger had developed a reputation as a collector of marked books as evidenced by this correspondence between N. M. Broadbent and Joseph Quincy Adams, who became director of the Folger Shakespeare Library in 1934.

V   *Ides hic, Spectator Candide, veram deli-*
neationem Bibliothecæ Publicæ celeberrimæ
Academiæ Lugduno-Batavæ, prout in usum
Reipublicæ (præcipue tamen Doctorum vi-
rorum & Studioforum publicitùs instituta
est: quæ ingenti numero variorum & insignium librorum

Itala quos tellus, quos quondam Græcia novit
Hos omnes doctos hic locus unus habet

Tgeologicorum, Iuridicorum, Medicorŭ, Philosophicorum,
Historicorum, Mathematicorum, aliarumque scientia-
rum & artium, ut etiam diversarŭ linguarum, Hebraicæ,
Chaldaicæ, Syriacæ, Arabicæ, Græcæ, Latinæ, Italicæ, Gal-
licæ, Hispanicæ, Germanicæ, Belgicæ, &c. egregie instructa
*   est.*

107

'Books . . . the frailest and tenderest matter . . . outlast brass, iron, and marble':
The Reader Revealed Through Collecting

The early modern reader is revealed to us today primarily through evidence in contemporary books and manuscripts. Accumulated and preserved by great libraries and individual collectors over the centuries, these books document the humble origins of a significant number of former owners and readers. The story revealed is an amazing and on-going saga of use, reverence, survival, and endurance.

107
Johannes van Meurs.
Illustrium Hollandiae & Westfrisiae Ordinum Alma Academia Leidensis.
Lugduni Batavorum, 1614.
Sigs. Ffiiv–Ffiiir
LF 4155 M4 1614 Cage

108
Thomas, à Kempis (1380–1471).
Opera et libri vite Fratris Thome de Kempis.
Colop: [Nuremberg], Per Caspar Hochfeder opifice accuratissime impressi, in vigilia Andree Ap[osto]i [29 Nov.] Anno [Christ]i, 1494.
Binding
INC T320

Medieval libraries often kept at least a portion of their books chained to shelves. The Leiden University Library (cat. no. 107), although founded in 1575, maintained the practice. The custom impeded the theft of valuable volumes and in some instances was used to create non-circulating reference collections of the most important works in any discipline. Chained books were shelved with the spines to the back to prevent tangling of the chains when one book was removed. This volume of Thomas à Kempis's *Works* has survived with part of its chain intact.

109
Great Britain. Court of Star Chamber.
A decree . . . concerning printing.
London, Robert Barker and by the assignes of Iohn Bill, 1637.
Sig. H4r
STC 7757

In 1610 Sir Thomas Bodley entered into an agreement with the Stationers' Company of London to receive one copy of every book printed by the Company's members for the Bodleian Library at Oxford. The agreement was renewed in this 1637 Star Chamber decree and in all successive licensing and copyright acts thereafter, making the Bodleian the first national depository library.

108

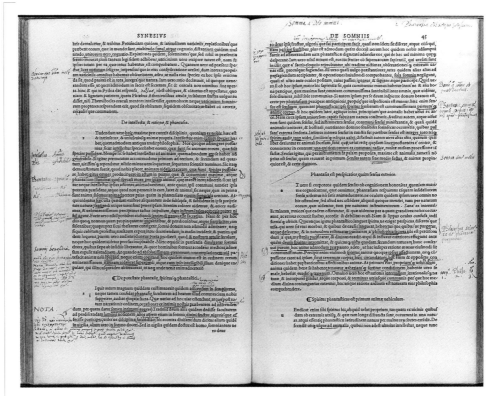

110

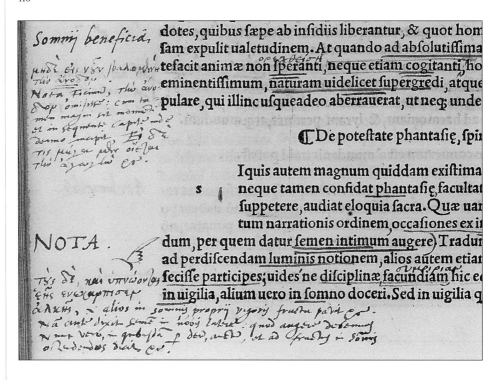

110 DETAIL

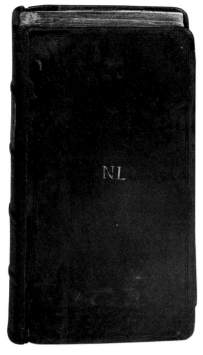

111

110
Marsilio Ficino (1433–1499).
De triplici vita.
(With, Jamblichus, *De mysteriis Aegyptiorum*,
and 19 other works).
Venitië, Erven Aldus Manutius en Andrea
Torresano, 1516.
Sigs. F4v–F5r
BF 1501 J2 Cage copy 2
Dee's signature illustrated on page 31.

By 1583 the Elizabethan mathematician and
astrologer John Dee had built a colossal library
of 3000–4000 volumes, nearly ten times the
size of other significant, contemporary private
collections. Dee acquired his books through
purchase, as gifts, and by failing to return
those he borrowed. His library was so large
that it required its own building at Mortlake.
When dispersed, it was the single largest infu-
sion of texts into the open market since the
Henrican dissolution of the monasteries.
Manuscript notes in most of the surviving
books Dee owned provide insight into how he
used them.

111
Giovanni Boccaccio (1313–1375).
*The modell of wit, mirth, eloquence
and conversation.*
London, By Tho. Cotes, and are to be sold by
Benjamine Allen and William Hope, 1634.
Binding
STC 3174 copy 2

Narcissus Luttrell, a noted late-seventeenth-
century collector of books and ephemera, personalized this binding with his initials. On the
title pages of many of his acquisitions, Luttrell
recorded the price, date of publication, and
occasional comments. Luttrell's abbreviated
signature and the year appear on the front
endleaf of this volume. Much of his collection
remained intact after his death, ending up in
the British Library, although some strayed
to other collections such as the Folger
Shakespeare Library. (See illus., page 76)

'This book, as long-liv'd as the elements': Whither Books and Readers?

The current era of rapidly changing media has provoked a great deal of anxiety and discussion about the future of books and reading as we know them. Will black ink impressed on wood-based paper arranged in codex form be supplanted by pixels on an LCD display? Is an interactive screen conducive to creating marginalia? Will the essence of today's readers survive in cyberspace? Gutenberg's innovations did not obliterate manuscript production, nor has e-media obliterated hand press production. While some current trends in alternative media have many practical uses, readers continue to be drawn to forms that appeal aesthetically and sensually, like fine paper and handcrafted human art, elements that are perhaps eternal.

112
Bible. Latin. ca. 1455.
Biblia latina. . .
[Mainz, ca. 1455].
Unfoliated leaf
INC B460

Gutenberg's Bible, a marvel in the fifteenth century, continues to be one of the world's most beautiful and valued books 500 years later. Although produced on a machine, this leaf from I Corinthians was lovingly decorated by hand. Gutenberg's printing blended technology and art into text that was accessible and appealing. This approach remains the foundation of modern book production.

113
Barry Moser.
[Test impression for the Pennyroyal-Caxton edition of the Holy Bible].
The first book of Moses called Genesis.
West Hatfield, MA, Pennyroyal-Caxton
Press, 1999.
Acc. 252206
The Gift of Heritage Bookshop

Amid the digital revolution, American 'book-smith' Barry Moser has created a spectacular handcrafted, extraillustrated edition of the Bible, the book which he points out has "been the crowning [masterpiece] of the world's great typographers, printers, and illustrators." Moser envisions this Bible, based on the King James Version, as "first and foremost a reading Bible; a Bible to be enjoyed as a book as well

as a sacred text." Produced using traditional methods and materials, this work is intended to last 500 years.

114
Gutenberg Digital. . . The Göttingen Gutenberg Bible [on CD-ROM].
München, K. G. Saur Electronic
Publishing, 2000.
Generously lent by Sabrina Alcorn Baron

115
The New Testament [on audio tape].
Indianapolis, IN, Faith Congregation
Outreach, [1990].
Generously lent by Laura Janis Hill

manifestū erit . Dies enim dñi declara=
bit:qa i igne reuelabit:z vniuscuiusqz
opus qle sit ignis pbabit . Bi cui⁹ o=
pus māserit qd supedificauit:mercedē
accipiet.Bi cui⁹ op⁹ arserit detrimetū
patiet:ipe aūt saluus erit:sic tame qli
p igne. Rescitis qa teplū dei estis:z spi=
rit⁹ dei habitat i vobis? Bi qs autem
teplū dei violauerit:dispdet illū deus.
Teplū eni dei sactū e: qd estis vos. Re=
mo se seducat. Bi qs videt iter vos sa=
piēs esse i hoc seclo:stult⁹ fiat ut sit sa=
piēs.Bapiētia eni hui⁹ mūdi stulticia
est apud deū.Scriptū est eni. Lōprehē=
dam sapientes in astutia eor . Et iterū.
De⁹ nouit cogitacōnes sapientū: qm
vane sūt. Remo itaqz glorietur in ho=
minibz.Oīa eni vra sūt:siue paul⁹
siue apollo siue cephas siue mund⁹
siue vita siue mors siue psentia siue fu=
tura . Omnia enim vestra sunt: vos
autem cristi:xpus autem dei.IIII

Sir nos existimet homo ut mini=
stros xpi:et dispesatores misterio=
rū dei.Hic ia queritr inter dispesatores:
ut fidelis qs iueniat. Michi aūt p mi=
nimo e ut a vobis iudicer: aut ab hu=
mano die . Bed neqz meipm iudico.
Richil eni michi cōsci⁹ sum: sed nō in
hoc iustificat⁹ sum. Qui aūt iudicat
me:dñs e. Itaqz nolite ate tempʼ iudi=
care:quoadusqz veniat dñs qui z illu=
minabit abscōdita tenebrax et mani=
festabit ōsilia cordiū: z tunc laus erit
vnicuiqz a deo.Hec aūt fres trāsfigura=
ui i me z apollo pter vos:ut i vobis
discatis ne supra quā scriptū est vn⁹
adūsus altez infletur p alio. Quis e=
nim te discernit? Quid aūt habes qd
nō accepisti? Bi aūt accepisti: qd glo=
riaris qsi nō acceperis? Iam saturati
estis:ia diuites facti estis.Bine nobis

regnatis.Et vinā regnetis: ut z nos
vobiscū regnem⁹.Puto eni qp deʼ nos
aplos nouissimos ostendit tāqz mor=
ti destinatos : qa spectacsin facti sum⁹
mūdo z āgelis et hominibz.Ros stul=
ti pter xpm: vos aūt prudetes i xpo.
Ros infirmi: vos aute fortes. Bos
nobiles:nos aūt ignobiles . Usqz in
hāc horā z esurim⁹ z sitim⁹ z nudi su=
mus:z colaphis cedimur z instabiles
sum⁹:z laboram⁹ operātes manibz no=
stris. Maledicimr: et bñdicim⁹. Perse=
cutōne patimr: et sustinem⁹. Blasphe=
mamr: z obsecram⁹. Tāqz purgameta
hui⁹ mūdi:facti sum⁹ oīū peripsima
usqz adhuc. Nō ut cōfundā vos hec scri=
bo: sed ut filios meos carissimos mo=
neo. Rā si dece milia pedagogox habe=
atis in xpo:sed nō mtros pres. Rā in
xpo ihesu p euangeliū ego vos genui.
Rogo ergo vos : imitatores mei esto=
te. Ideo misi ad vos thimotheū qi e fi=
li⁹ me⁹ carissim⁹ z fidelis i dño:qi vos
cōmonefaciat vias meas qi sūt in xpo
ihesu: sicut vbiqz i oīm ecclesia doceo.
Tāqz nō veturʼ sim ad vos:sicut infla=
ti sūt quidā. Veniā aūt ad vos cito si
dñs voluerit:z cognoscā nō sermonē e=
orū qi inflati sūt: sed virtute. Nō eni i
sermone e regnū dei:sed i virtute.Quid
vultis? In virga veniā ad vos-an in
caritate z spiritu māsuetudinis?

Omnino auditr iter vos fornica=
tio:z talis fornicatio qlis nec in=
ter gētes:ita ut vxorē pris sui aliqs ha=
beat.Et vos inflati estis:z nō magis
luctū habuistis:ut tollat de medio ve=
strū qi hoc op⁹ fecit. Ego quidē absens
corpore-psens aūt spiritu: ia iudicaui
ut psens eū qi sic operat⁹ e in noie dñi
nri ihesu xpi cōgregatis vobis et meo
spiritu cū virtute domini ihesu tradere

Select Bibliography

Altick, Richard Daniel. *The English Common Reader: A Social History of the Mass Reading Public, 1800–1900*. Chicago, IL: University of Chicago Press, 1957.

Amman, Jost, and Hans Sachs. *The Book of Trades [Standebuch]*. With a new introduction by Benjamin A. Rifkin. New York: Dover Publications, 1973.

Battigelli, Anna. *Margaret Cavendish and the Exiles of the Mind*. Lexington, KY: University Press of Kentucky, 1998.

Beal, Peter. *In Praise of Scribes*. Oxford: Oxford University Press, 1998.

Beale, Joseph Henry. *A Bibliography of Early English Law Books*. Cambridge, MA: Harvard University Press, 1926.

Bearman, Frederick A., Nati H. Krivatsy, and J. Franklin Mowery. *Fine and Historic Bookbindings from the Folger Shakespeare Library*. Washington, DC: Folger Shakespeare Library, 1992.

Benedict, Barbara M. *Making the Modern Reader: Cultural Mediation in Early Modern Literary Anthologies*. Princeton, NJ: Princeton University Press, 1996.

Bennett, H. S. *English Books & Readers 1603–1640: Being a study in the History of the Book Trade in the Reigns of James I and Charles I*. Cambridge: Cambridge University Press, 1970.

Bibliopola: Bilder und Texte aus der Welt des Buchhandels. Pictures and texts about the book trade. Images et texte sur la librarie. Sigfried Taubert, Roy Giles, Frederick Plaat, and Bernard Ernst, eds. 2 vols. Hamburg: E. Hauswedell, [1966].

Birkerts, Sven. *The Gutenberg Elegies: The Fate of Reading in an Electronic Age*. Boston and London: Faber and Faber, 1994.

Blayney, Peter W. M. *The Bookshops in Paul's Cross Churchyard*. Occasional Papers of The Bibliographical Society, 5. London: The Bibliographical Society, 1990.

Blayney, Peter W. M. *The First Folio of Shakespeare*. Washington, DC: Folger Shakespeare Library, 1991.

Blayney, Peter W. M. "The Publication of Playbooks." In *A New History of Early English Drama*. John D. Cox and David Scott Kastan, eds. New York: Columbia University Press, 1997.

Bliss, Carey S. *Some Aspects of Seventeenth-Century English Printing with Special Reference to Joseph Moxon*. Los Angeles, CA: William Andrews Clark Memorial Library, 1965.

Bowen, Dorothy. *The Book of Common Prayer: The James R. Page Collection*. Los Angeles, CA: The Plantin Press, 1953.

Brook, G. L. *Books and Book-Collecting*. London: Andre Deutsch, 1980.

Brown, Cedric, and Arthur Marotti. *Text and Cultural Change in Early Modern England*. New York: St. Martin's Press, 1997.

Brown, Michelle P. *The British Library Guide to Writing and Scripts*. Toronto: University of Toronto Press, 1998.

Bühler, Curt. *The Fifteenth-Century Book: The Scribes. The Printers. The Decorators*. Philadelphia, PA: University of Pennsylvania Press, 1960.

Burke, Redmond A. *What is the INDEX?* Milwaukee, WI: Bruce Publishing, 1952.

Capp, Bernard S. *English Almanacs, 1500–1800: Astrology and the Popular Press*. Ithaca, NY: Cornell University Press, 1979.

Carvalho, David N. *Forty Centuries of Ink*. New York, 1904.

Chartier, Roger. *The Order of Books*. Stanford, CA: Stanford University Press, 1994.

Clapp, Sarah. "The Subscription Enterprises of John Ogilby and Richard Blome." *Modern Philology* 30 (1933).

Coleman, Janet. *Medieval Readers and Writers, 1350–1400*. New York: Columbia University Press, 1981.

Corbett, Margery, and Ronald Lightbown. *The Comely Frontispiece: the Emblematic Title-Page in England 1550–1660*. London: Routledge & Kegan Paul, 1979.

Cressy, David. *Literacy and the Social Order: Reading and Writing in Tudor and Stuart England*. Cambridge: Cambridge University Press, 1980.

The Culture of Print: Power and the Uses of Print in Early Modern Europe. Roger Chartier, ed. Lydia G. Cochrane, trans. Oxford: The Clarendon Press, 1989.

Darnton, Robert. *The Kiss of Lamourette: Reflections in Cultural History*. Boston and London: Faber and Faber, 1990.

DeGrazia, Diane. *Prints and Related Drawings by the Carracci family: a catalogue raisonné*. Washington, DC: National Gallery of Art, 1979.

DeRicci, Seymour. *English Collectors of Books and Manuscripts, 1530–1930*. Cambridge: Cambridge University Press, 1930.

DeStrata, Filippo. *Polemic Against Printing*. Shelagh Grier and Martin Lowry, eds. The Hayloft Press, 1986.

Dreyfus, John. "The Invention of Spectacles and the Advent of Printing." *The Library* 6th ser., 10 (1988).

Eisenstein, Elizabeth L. *The Printing Press as an Agent of Change*. Cambridge: Cambridge University Press, 1979; repr. 1997.

English Historical Scholarship in the Sixteenth and Seventeenth Centuries. Levi Fox, ed. London: Oxford University Press, 1956.

"English Monarchs and Their Books: From Henry VII to Charles II." Exhibition notes, British Library, 20 November 1986–15 February 1987.

Ferguson, W. Craig. *Pica Roman Type in Elizabethan England*. Aldershot: Scolar Press, 1989.

Fevre, Lucien, and Henri-Jean Martin. *The Coming of the Book: The Impact of Printing 1450–1800*. D. Gerard, trans. London and New York: Verso, 1990.

Gainsford, Thomas. *Vox Spiritus, or Sir Walter Rawleigh's Ghost*. Exeter: The Rota at the University of Exeter, 1983.

G. D.'s Direction for Writing set forth for the benefit of poore scholers now reprinted from the sole surviving copy published in London A.D. 1656. Cambridge: Cambridge University Press, 1933.

Grafton, Anthony. *Commerce with the Classics: Ancient Books and Renaissance Readers*. Ann Arbor, MI: University of Michigan Press, 1997.

Green, I. M. *The Christian's ABC: Catechisms and Catechizing in England c. 1530–1740*. Oxford: The Clarendon Press, 1996.

Gregg, Pauline. *Free-Born John: A Biography of John Lilburne*. London and Melbourne: J. M. Dent and Sons, 1986.

Gumbert, J. P. "Typography in the manuscript book," *Journal of the Printing Historical Society* 22 (1993).

Gutenberg, Man of the Millennium: From a secret enterprise to the first media revolution. City of Mainz, 2000.

Hamburger, Philip. "The Development of the Law of Seditious Libel and the Control of the Press." *Stanford Law Review* 37 (1985).

Heal, Ambrose. *The English Writing-Masters and Their Copy Books, 1570–1800.* Cambridge: Cambridge University Press, 1931.

A History of Reading in the West. Gugliemo Cavallo and Roger Chartier, eds. Lydia G. Cochrane, trans. Amherst, MA: University of Massachusetts Press, 1999.

Hulvey, Monique. "Not so Marginal: Manuscript Annotations in the Folger Incunabula," *The Papers of the Bibiliographical Society of America* 92 (1998).

Imagination on a Long Rein: English Literature Illustrated. Joachim Möller, ed. Marburg: Verlag, 1988.

Index of English Literary Manuscripts. Vol. I: 1450–1625. Comp. Peter Beal. London and New York: Mansell, 1980.

Janson, W. H. *Apes and Ape Lore in the Middle Ages and the Renaissance.* London: Warburg Institute, 1952.

Jardine, Lisa, and Anthony Grafton. "'Studied for Action': How Gabriel Harvey Read His Livy." *Past & Present* no. 129 (1990).

John Gay Poetry and Prose. Vol. II. Ed. Vinton A. Dearing. Oxford: The Clarendon Press, 1974.

John Gay's Fables (1727, 1738). Ed. and intro. by Vinton A. Dearing. Los Angeles, CA: William Andrews Clark Memorial Library, 1967.

Johnson, Greg. "Drawing on Holy Writ." *Spectator* (Winter 2000).

Kendrick, Laura. *Animating the Letter: the figurative embodiment of writing from late antiquity to the Renaissance.* Columbus, OH: Ohio State University Press, [1999].

Kintgen, Eugene R. *Reading in Tudor England.* Pittsburgh, PA: University of Pittsburgh Press, [1996].

Krivatsy, Nati. *Bibliography of the Works of Gregorio Leti.* New Castle, DE: Oak Knoll Press, 1982.

Landwehr, John. *Books in the Low Countries, 1554–1949: A Bibliography.* Utrecht, 1970.

Lee, Brian North. *Early Printed Book Labels.* Penner, Mdx.: Private Libraries Association and The Bookplate Society, 1976.

Love, Harold. *Scribal Publication in Seventeenth-Century England.* Oxford: The Clarendon Press, 1993.

Lucas, Peter J. "Sixteenth-Century English Spelling Reform and the Printers in Continental Perspective: Sir Thomas Smith and John Hart." *The Library* 7th ser, 1 (March 2000).

Manguel, Alberto. *A History of Reading.* London: Flamingo, 1996.

Marotti, Arthur. *Manuscript, Print, and the English Renaissance Lyric.* London and Ithaca: Cornell University Press, 1995.

Martin, Henri-Jean. *The History and Power of Writing.* Lydia G. Cochrane, trans. Chicago, IL: University of Chicago Press, 1994.

McKenzie, D. F. *The London Book Trade in the Later-Seventeenth Century.* Sandars Lectures, 1976.

McKenzie, D. F. "Printers of the Mind: Some Notes on Bibliographical Theories and Printing-House Practices." *Studies in Bibliography* 22 (1969).

McPherson, David. "Ben Jonson's Library and Marginalia." *Studies in Philology* 71 (Dec. 1974).

Mendle, Michael. "A Machiavellian in the Long Parliament before the Civil War." *Parliamentary History* 8 (1989).

Milton, John. *AREOPAGITICA; A SPEECH OF Mr. JOHN MILTON For the Liberty of VNLICENC'D PRINTING, To the PARLIA-MENT of ENGLAND*. London, Printed in the Yeare, 1644.

Morison, Stanley. *English Prayer Books.* Cambridge: Cambridge University Press, 1949.

Morison, Stanley. *Politics and Script: Aspects of Authority and Freedom in the Development of Politics and Script from the Sixth Century B.C. to the Twentieth Century A.D.* Oxford: The Clarendon Press, 1972.

Noakes, David. *John Gay. A Profession of Friendship.* Oxford: Oxford University Press, 1995.

New Ways of Looking at Old Texts: Papers of the Renaissance English Text Society, 1985–1991. W. Speed Hill, ed. Binghamton, NY: Medieval and Renaissance Texts and Studies, 1993.

Of the Making of Books: Medieval Manuscripts, Their Scribes and Readers. P. R. Robinson and Rivkah Zim, eds. Brookfield, VT: Ashgate, 1997.

Ola, Per, and Emily D'Aulaire. "Inscribing the Word." *Smithsonian Magazine* (December 2000).

Olmert, Michael. *The Smithsonian Book of Books.* Washington, DC: Smithsonian Institution, 1992.

Olson, David R. *The World on Paper: the conceptual and cognitive implications of writing and reading.* Cambridge: Cambridge University Press, 1994.

Ong, Walter J. *Orality and Literacy: the technology of the word.* London and New York: Methuen, 1982.

Orme, Nicholas. *Early British Swimming, 55 BC–AD 1719.* Exeter, 1983.

Parkes, M. B. *Pause and Effect: an introduction to the history of punctuation in the west.* Berkeley and Los Angeles, CA: University of California Press, [1993].

Parkes, M.B. *Scribes, Scripts, and Readers: Studies in the Communication, Presentation, and Dissemination of Medieval Texts.* London and Rio Grande, OH: Hambledon Press, 1991.

Parry, Graham. *The Trophies of Time: English Antiquarians of the Seventeenth Century.* Oxford: Oxford University Press, 1995.

Pennyroyal Press. "THE HOLY BIBLE: An Illustrated Folio Edition of the King James Bible to be published in 1999." www.pennyroyalcaxton.com-prospectus.

The Politics of Information in Early Modern Europe. Brendan M. Dooley and Sabrina A. Baron, eds. London: Routledge, 2001.

Praz, Mario. *Studies in Seventeenth-Century Imagery.* 2nd ed. Rome, 1964.

Pressly, William L. *A Catalogue of Paintings in the Folger Shakespeare Library. "As Imagination Bodies Forth."* London and New Haven: Yale University Press, 1993.

Printing the Written Word: The Social History of Books, circa 1450–1520. Sandra Hindman, ed. Ithaca, NY: Cornell University Press, 1991.

Private Libraries in Renaissance England: A Collection and Catalogue of Tudor and Early Stuart Book-Lists. Vol. I. Robert J. Fehrenbach, gen. ed. E. S. Leedham-Green, UK ed. Binghamton, NY: Medieval and Renaissance Texts and Studies; Marlborough, England: Adam Matthew Publications, 1992.

Realms of Gold: Books and Libraries in the Renaissance. Folger Shakespeare Library Exhibition, April 1981–April 1982.

Reed, John Curtis. "Humphrey Moseley, publisher." *Proceedings & Papers of the Oxford Bibliographical Society* 2 (1927–30).

The Reformation and the Book. Jean-Francois Gilmont, ed. Karin Maag, trans. Brookfield, VT: Ashgate, 1998.

The Renaissance Text: Theory, Editing, Textuality. Andrew Murphy, ed. Manchester: Manchester University Press, 2000.

Richardson, Brian. *Printing, Writers, and Readers in Renaissance Italy.* New York: Cambridge University Press, 1999.

Rosenthal, Bernard M. *The Rosenthal Collection of Printed Books with Manuscript Annotations.* New Haven, CT: Yale University Press, 1997.

Rothstein, Marian. *Reading in the Renaissance: Amadis de Gaule and the Lessons of Memory.* Newark, DE: University of Delaware Press, [1999].

The Royal Exchange. Ann Saunders, ed. London: The London Topographical Society, 1997.

Scarisbrick, Diana. *Jewelry in Britain, 1066–1837: a documentary, social, literary, and artistic survey.* Wilby: M. Russell, 1994.

Shenkeveld, Maria A. *Dutch Literature in the Age of Rembrandt.* Amsterdam and Philadelphia, J. Benjamins, 1991.

Schoenbaum, S. *Shakespeare, The Globe & The World.* New York: Folger Shakespeare Library and Oxford University Press, 1979.

Shuchard, Margret. *A Descriptive Bibliography of the Works of John Ogilby and William Morgan.* Bern and Frankfurt am Main: European University Papers, 1975.

Scott-Elliott, A. H., and Elspeth Yeo. "Calligraphic Manuscripts of Esther Inglis (1571–1624): A Catalogue." *The Papers of the Bibliographical Society of America* 84 (1990).

Sharpe, Kevin M. *Reading Revolutions: The Politics of Reading in Early Modern England.* London and New Haven: Yale University Press, 2000.

Sherman, Claire Richter. *Writing on Hands: Memory and Knowledge in Early Modern Europe.* Carlisle, PA: The Trout Gallery, Dickinson College, [2000].

Sherman, William H. *John Dee: The Politics of Reading and Writing in the English Renaissance.* Amherst, MA: University of Massachusetts Press, 1995.

Shesgren, Sean. "The Cries of London in the Seventeenth Century." *The Papers of the Bibliographical Society of America* 86 (1992).

Shevelow, Kathryn. *Women and Print Culture: the Construction of Femininity in the Early Modern Periodical.* London and New York: Routledge, 1989.

Sinfield, Alan. *Faultlines: Cultural Materialism and the Politics of Dissident Reading.* Berkeley and Los Angeles, CA: University of California Press, [1992].

Smedley, W. T. *The Mystery of Francis Bacon.* London: Robert Banks & Son, 1912.

Spufford, Margaret. *Small Books and Pleasant Histories: Popular Fiction and Its Readership in Seventeenth-Century England.* Athens, GA: University of Georgia Press, 1981.

Thomas, Sir Keith. "The Meaning of Literacy in Early Modern England." In *The Written Word: Literacy in Transition.* Gerd Baumann, ed. Oxford: Oxford University Press, 1986.

Thomas-Stanford, Charles. *Early Editions of Euclid's Elements*. London: The Bibliographical Society, 1926.

Tjan-Bakker, Anneke. "Dame Flora's Blossoms: Esther Inglis's Flower-Illustrated Manuscripts." *English Manuscript Studies* 9 (2000).

Tottel's Miscellany. Ed. Hyder Edward Rollins. 2 vols., rev. ed. Cambridge, MA: Harvard University Press, 1965.

Twyman, Michael. *The British Library Guide to Printing*. Toronto: University of Toronto Press, 1999.

Tribble, Evelyn B. *Margins and Marginality: The Printed Page in Early Modern England*. Charlottesville, VA: University Press of Virginia, 1993.

2,000 years of Calligraphy: A Comprehensive Catalogue. Baltimore, MD: The Baltimore Museum of Art, The Peabody Institute Library, and The Walters Art Gallery, 1965.

The Universal Penman: A Survey of Western Calligraphy from the Roman Period to 1980. Joyce Irene Whalley and Vera C. Kaden, eds. London: HMSO, 1980.

Van Eerde, Katherine E. *John Ogilby and the Taste of His Times*. Folkestone, Kent: William Dawson & Sons, 1976.

Vives, Juan Luis. *The Education of a Christian Woman: A Sixteenth-Century Manual*. Ed. and trans. Charles Fantazzi. Chicago, IL: University of Chicago Press, 2000.

Women, Writing, and the Reproduction of Culture in Tudor and Stuart Britain. Mary E. Burke, Jane Donawerth, Linda L. Dove, and Karen Nelson, eds. Syracuse, NY: Syracuse University Press, 2000.

Woolf, Daniel R. *Reading History in Early Modern England*. Cambridge and New York: Cambridge University Press, 2000.

Woodhuysen, H. R. *Sir Philip Sidney and the Circulation of Manuscripts, 1558–1640*. Oxford: The Clarendon Press, 1996.

Ziegler, Georgianna. "Hand-Ma[I]de Books: The Manuscripts of Esther Inglis, Early-Modern Precursors of the Artist's Book." *English Manuscript Studies* 9 (2000).

Notes on Contributors

Jennifer Andersen teaches English and Latin at California State University, San Bernadino. She is co-editor with Elizabeth Sauer of *Books and Readers in Early Modern England* (forthcoming, 2001). Her current research is on "Pamphlet Genres in Early Modern England."

Sabrina Alcorn Baron teaches History at the University of Maryland, Baltimore County. She is co-editor with Brendan M. Dooley of *The Politics of Information in Early Modern Europe* (2001). Her current research is on "Licensing for the Press in Sixteenth- and Seventeenth-Century England."

Anna Battigelli teaches English at the State University of New York, Plattsburgh. She is the author of *Margaret Cavendish and the Exiles of the Mind* (1998) which was selected as a *Choice* Outstanding Title. She has also published on John Dryden and his circle.

Anthony Grafton teaches History at Princeton University. He is the author of, among other works, *Defenders of the Text* (1991) and *The Footnote: A Curious History* (1997).

Arthur F. Marotti teaches English at Wayne State University. He is the author most recently of *Manuscript, Print, and the English Renaissance Lyric* (1995); editor most recently of *Catholicism and Anti-Catholicism in Early Modern English Texts* (1999); and co-editor with Michael Bristol of *Print, Manuscript and Performance: The Changing Relations of the Media in Early Modern England* (2000). He is completing a book entitled *Catholic and Anti-Catholic Discourses in Early Modern England*.

Kevin Sharpe teaches Renaissance Studies at the Centre for Renaissance Studies, Department of English, University of Warwick. He is the author most recently of *Reading Revolutions: The Politics of Reading in Early Modern England* (2000). His current research is on "Representations of Authority and Images of Power, 1500-1700."

William H. Sherman teaches English at the University of Maryland, College Park. He is the author of *John Dee: The Politics of Reading and Writing in the English Renaissance* (1995). His current research is on "Marginalia in Renaissance Books."

Evelyn B. Tribble teaches English at Temple University. She is the author of *Margins and Marginality: The Printed Page in Early Modern England* (1993). Her current research is on "Technologies of Writing from Plato to the Digital Age."

Steven N. Zwicker teaches English at Washington University in St. Louis. He is the author of *Lines of Authority* (1993) and most recently co-editor with Kevin M. Sharpe of *Refiguring Revolutions: Aesthetics and Politics from the English Revolution to The Romantic Revolution* (2000). His current research is on "Habits of Reading in Early Modern England."